Exploring Shawl Shapes
27 Mini Shawls to Knit

Elizabeth Lovick

Cover and Page Design
Judith Brodnicki

Technical Editor
Elly Doyle

Northern Lace Press

Flotta — Orkney — Scotland

Exploring Shawl Shapes: 27 Mini Shawls to Knit

ISBN: 978-0-9930614-7-9

Published May 2015 by Northern Lace Press,
Orkney (UK)

Northern Lace Press

Flotta — Orkney — Scotland

www.northernlacepress.co.uk

Why a book for Mini Shawls?

Over the years I have designed mini shawls for workshops, and they have always proved popular. I have often been asked to collect them together, so that is what I have done.

In addition, I have designed minis for all the popular shawl shapes, and have tried to show some of the ways in which each shape can be achieved. The Regional section gives a pattern for each area which is knitted in the traditional way, and the Extra Patterns gives some other ideas of possible shapes and uses.

In many cases, the patterns can be expanded to full sized shawls, and I have given notes to help you do this.

Whether you knit the shawls to help you understand their construction, or whether you knit them because you like the pattern, I hope you will enjoy exploring the shawl shapes here.

Elizabeth Lovick
May 2015

But What Can I DO With Them?

Some folk like to knit mini shawls for the fun of it. Others need an end use. Here are some things you can do with your finished minis.

- shawls for dolls and teddies
- make them in cotton as wash cloths and dish cloths
- mats for the table or dressing table
- tray cloths
- work the 'squares' longer as scarves
- work them in thick yarns as small shawls
- cushion covers
- appliqué them to cushions or quilts
- frame them and hang them on the wall as the Art they are!

Contents

General Information for All Patterns

Notes

All patterns need a row counter and tapestry needle to complete them. This is not mentioned in the materials list.

Needle lengths are not specified as this is very much a question of preference, and whether you use a "magic loop."

Tension is always after washing and dressing/blocking.

Tension not critical, but if your tension is looser than specified, your piece will be bigger, and it will use more yarn. Similarly, if you use a thick yarn than that specified you will need a longer yardage.

The stitch left after casting off is included in following figure.

Stitch markers are only mentioned when important. At other times slip them when you come to them.

Abbreviations

G2 - gather 2 by knitting the next 2 sts together, leaving them on the needle, then knitting them together through the back of the loops. 2 sts are used and 2 are formed.

st(s) - stitch(es)

k - knit

kfb - knit into the front, then the back, of the next stitch (so increasing 1 st)

ktb - knit the last stich of the lace togehter with the next stitch of the border

k2tog - knit next two stitches together

k2togtbl - knit 3 sts together through the back of the loops

k3tog - knit next three stitches together

k5togtbl - knit 5 sts together through the back of the loops

M - marker

m1 - make 1

p - purl

PM - place marker

s1p - slip the next st purl-wise

SM - slip marker

ssk - slip the next 2 sts onto the other needle knitwise; put them back then knit them together

MN - make nupp as follows: in the next stitch (k1, yo, k1, yo, k1, yo, k1), that is 7 loops in the one stitch. On the NEXT row, PURL the 7 sts together.

yo - yarn over needle

Charts

Most of the charts are based on garter stitch, so a blank square is always knit and a square with a dot is always purl UNLESS the pattern says otherwise.

Some charts have every row charted; others chart only odd numbered rows. Each chart specifies which notation is being used, and if only odd numbered rows are charted, how to work even numbered rows is also noted.

Charts are worked from the bottom up. Odd numbered rows are worked from right to left. Even numbered rows, if charted, are worked from left to right.

(See also Working with Charts on page 19.)

Chart Symbols Key

	knit
•	purl
O	yo
/	odd rows: k2tog; even rows: ssk/k2togtbl
\	odd rows: ssk/k2togtbl; even rows: k2tog
▲	k3togtbl
$	s1p
✻	ktb
/5\	k5togtbl
⤬	G2
〰	nupp
V	kfb
⌒	cast off

What Yarn to Use?

Any yarn can be used for a lace project – but some will work better than others. You can use anything from a super-chunky to frog hair. HOWEVER, different yarns do work better in different circumstances. For mini shawls your yarn choice is not as critical as for a full sized shawl, but it is worth thinking about whether a particular yarn is likely to work.

There are three things you need to think about:

- Thickness
- Fibre Content
- Colour

YARN THICKNESS

In general, the heavier wear a piece will get, the heavier the yarn. It is POSSIBLE to knit a throw for the cat's couch out of gossamer thread, but it isn't necessarily SENSIBLE.

The Yarn Thickness Chart (at right) will give some idea of what might be worth using for what. It isn't set in stone, but it will give you an idea where to start.

This list is not exhaustive – it is just to give you some idea what weight of yarn might work for a particular project, and what project might work for a particular yarn.

YARN COMPOSITION

Once again, you CAN do anything with anything, but your sanity might be saved if you think a bit first.

YARN THICKNESS AND RECOMMENDED USES

Yarn Thickness	Use for
Thicker than aran	Throws, knee rugs, heavy winter scarves
Aran	Throws, bed spreads, scarves, cushion covers
DK	Baby blankets, cushion covers, scarves, heavy winter shawls
4 ply / fingering	Winter shawls, scarves, cowls / snoods, baby shawls for using, day sweaters and shrugs, socks, hats and gloves
2 ply / lace weight	Summer shawls, scarves, cowls/ snoods/mobius, table runners, doilies, table cloths, evening sweaters and shrugs, socks, hats and gloves
1 ply / cobweb	Wedding wear, baby shawls for keeping rather than wearing, table runners, doilies, table cloths
Thinner than 1 ply	Show-off items

> REMEMBER:
> If you are knitting to give away,
> a good acrylic is far better than a poor wool.

You need to think about the USE to which the final item will be put – in particular, how often will it be washed, and by whom? You might want to knit a cobweb cashmere or merino baby jacket, but mums rarely have the time or energy to hand wash and to take care of fine lace.

See the table on the next page for a quick look at the pros and cons of various yarn weights.

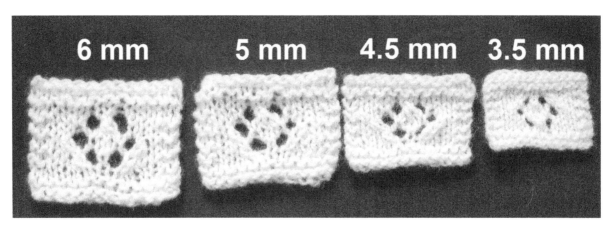

Photo 1: The same 4 ply / fingering weight knitted into the same pattern with different sized needles

Pros and Cons of Different Fibres for Lace Knitting

FIBRE	PROs	CONs	GOOD FOR
Acrylic and polyester	Strong fibres Easy care	Low snob value Some can stain easily	Baby clothes Wearing shawls Anything needing a lot of washing
Cotton and linen	Very strong fibres Dyes tend to be colourfast Can be washed at high temperatures	No drape, no memory, no give Very unforgiving Heavy for its size	Household items Light weight summer clothes
Silk	Strong fibres Takes dye very well	Can be slippery to work with Can be difficult to care for	Household items Shawls
Wool	Very forgiving Blocks well Drapes well Takes dye well	Not very easy to wash and dry Can be attacked by moths etc Relatively weak	Shawls Heirloom baby items Scarves, etc Throws
Alpaca	Very warm Drapes well	Heavy for size Not easy to care for No memory, can have halo	Wearing shawls Scarves etc
Mohair	Very light and warm	Halo can detract from pattern Not easy care	Shawls Scarves Light-weight tops
Cashmere	Very light and warm Forgiving Drapes well	Can be difficult to care for Relatively weak	Shawls Scarves, etc Sweaters, etc
Blends	In general, a blend of fibres will give you a yarn with the best of each fibre. So a cashmere/silk blend will be stronger than cashmere and more forgiving than silk		
'Superwash' fibres	Beware of anything labeled superwash! It might be OK, but it might end up like string. Also be aware that different washing machines are VERY different – and don't necessarily believe the washing instructions on the ball band. At very least read the small print carefully – usually 'machine washable' means in a washing machine at 30° C on a delicates setting NOT in with the normal wash.		

RECOMMENDED NEEDLE SIZES FOR DIFFERENT YARN THICKNESSES

Remember, these are starting points. You may want to use thinner or thicker needles for your yarn.

Yarn Thickness	UK Needle Size	US Needle Size
Chunky	10 to 15 mm	15 +
Aran	7 to 10 mm	10.5 to 15
DK	6 to 7 mm	10 to 10.5
4 ply / fingering	4.5 to 6 mm	7 to 10

Yarn Thickness	UK Needle Size	US Needle Size
3 ply / sock	4 to 5 mm	6 to 8
2 ply / lace weight	3.5 to 4.5 mm	4 to 7
1 ply cobweb	2.5 to 3.5 mm	1 to 4
finer	2 to 3 mm	1 to 2

Mini shawls can often be made from odds and ends of yarn. Most solid colours work well, and so do semi-solids. But beware of space-dyed yarns, especially sock yarns or others designed to give a 'fair isle' effect. The combination of short lengths of colour with patterns of holes usually mean that both get lost. Long colour repeats can look good, but at least think about the interaction of the chosen design with the chosen yarn before you start.

What Tension to Use?

Sometimes a pattern will look awful knitted with the wrong tension and stunning knitted either a lot tighter or a lot looser.

More often, the final effect is a matter of personal choice. There is no right and wrong – just different. Only you know what visual effect you are after, and how you like to knit. You do need to take some account of what the piece is for (you need to be able to see through a wedding veil) but apart from that, it is very much a case of personal choice.

As with all knitting, tension is all important - or rather, a consistent tension makes for a good looking piece. When doing a yarn-over, don't pull the yarn too tightly. These are supposed to be holes!

Make sure that you don't work too tightly. To start with, you may well find you do – simply because you are trying too hard! Relax, and treat it as any other knitting. At the same time, don't try to knit loosely. If you do, you will find you remember, forget, remember, forget – and as a result the piece will have lots of tension changes.

Because you are thinking about it, to begin with you may find that your tension is very uneven. Don't worry – tension differences are not so visible in lacy knitting as they are in stocking stitch. And as you relax you will find that you are getting a more even tension.

HAVE FAITH!

Any lace knitting before it is washed is scraggy and uninteresting. Once you wash it and dress/block it, the beauty suddenly becomes apparent. Once your swatches are dry, put them where you can see them (pinning them to a cork board is ideal). NOW is the time to decide exactly what is right!

Techniques

PROVISIONAL CAST ON

This is a method of casting on with a different yarn. It is used where stitches will later be picked up and is much more elastic than simply picking up cast on stitches.

The waste yarn is ideally thinner than the working yarn, and a different colourt. It should also be a smooth, non-sticky yarn. I use crochet cotton, here the yellow thread.

There are several methods of doing this, but the simplest is to cast on with the waste yarn, then continue with the working yarn.

Photo 2: Cast-on with waste yarn (gold); then start Row 1 with wo king yarn (blue)

CAST ON INTO A RING

There are several different ways of casting on for a circular shawl, depending on the effect you want. Which ever you use, be prepared to try several times before you get it right!!

Personally, I wrap a spare piece of the main yarn round my fingers, then using the main yarn I do the under-and-over cast on shown below:

At a later stage, the spare yarn ring can be tightened and the ends woven in.

A similar method is to use a crochet hook to make the right number of loops into the ring, and then to pick up the tops of the stitches with the needles.

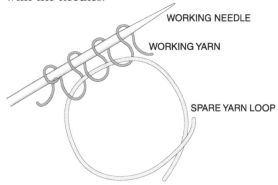

WORKING NEEDLE

WORKING YARN

SPARE YARN LOOP

LIFELINES

A lifeline is a fine thread which is run through every stitch on a row, and provides a row to take the work back to if you make a large mistake. Fine crochet cotton is also good for lifelines, as is strong sewing thread. Some folk use fishing line or other nylon line, but this can be harsh on very fine yarns.

Edges and Seams

On most lace pieces the edges of your knitting are on show. On scarves, shawls and stoles the edge of the piece can form an important part of the design, and it is worth taking a bit of time deciding what you are going to do about the edging. Here are three ways of dealing with this – which you use is up to you.

A) KNIT AND TUG

Knit the first stitch of the new row, then give the yarn a good tug – a really good tug, not a half hearted one. This tightens both the first stitch of the new and the last stitch of the old row. If you are afraid that the yarn might break, test its breaking strength on a spare bit of yarn.

Photo 3: Knit-and-tug edge

B) SLIP 1 PURLWISE

This gives a chain edge. It is very useful if you are going to pick up the stitches of that edge later.

Photo 4: S1p edge

C) YO, K2TOGTBL

Here you put the yarn over the needle as if to purl before you knit the first two stitches together through the back of the loops. This gives a small loop of yarn at the edge. It is worth noting that yarn over needle is the same as needle UNDER yarn. So you actually scoop the needle under the yarn as you put it into the first two stitches for the k2togtbl. Only use this edging with garter stitch.

Photo 5: Yo, k2togtbl edge

I suggest you knit a swatch and then pick up the edges to see which you like. Cast on 15 sts and work in all knit. Knit the first stitch of odd numbered rows, and work s1p at the start of even numbered row. After ten or twelve rows, change one to yo, k2togtbl. You can then see which effect you like best, or find easiest to do.

Picking Up Stitches

If you are picking up round a square you have three types of edges - the live stitches you have been knitting with, the cast on edge, and the two side edges. The way you pick up stitches is different for each. Always pick up with a needle considerably smaller than the one you are using. For fine yarns you might want to pick up with a tapestry needle and contrasting thread, and then transfer the stitches to your working needle.

A) CAST ON EDGE

How you pick this up depends on how you cast on. If you look at both sides of your cast on, you will see somewhere a line of slanting loops, one per stitch. Sometimes there are two per stitch, but one of them stays within the stitch and the other moves to the next stitch. This is the one you want. You are going to insert your needle across the slant of the loop, making an X with it. This makes it

Photo 6: Picking up stitches along the cast on edge

easier to then move the tip back to scoop up the next stitch.

The first and last stitch may have a different structure. This is where you improvise, and shove the needle through a knot!! Or you can just knit into the front and back of the stitch before.

B) PROVISIONAL CAST ON EDGE

Here you want to pick up the first row of loops from the working yarn, taking the loops behind the provision cast on stitches.

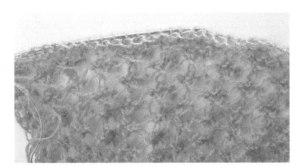

Photo 7: Picking up stitches along the provisional cast-on edge

C) KNITTED EDGE

If you look at the edge of your knitting, you will see a series of 'knots' joined by 'strands'. Each represents a row. As you are wanting to pick up one stitch for every two rows in garter stitch, you are going to pick up every knot. It is also possible to pick up the

Photo 8: Picking up stitches along the knitted edge

strands instead of the knots. However, it is more difficult to scoop up the lines, and the knots can show as bumps between the picked-up stitches.

For stocking stitch you again have knots and lines representing the rows. This time, however, you want to pick up roughly 3 stitches for every 4 rows. This means that as well as the knots, you are going to want a stitch in every other strand. These can be picked up as you go along OR, better, pick them up and knit them as you knit the picked up stitches. This latter way is easier, but does require a bit more concentration.

D) SLIP 1 EDGE

This looks like a chain, and for a garter stitch ground you are going to pick up one stitch from each chain. Each loop of the chain has 2 'legs'. If you pick up one leg, you will get a line on the finished piece where the other leg lies. If you pick up both legs, you will get a rather bulky 'seam'. Picking up both legs is also awkward. Pick up your 'leg' as you did for the cast on edge – inserting the needle to make an X.

Photo 9: Picking up stitches along the S1p edge

E) YO, K2TOGTBL EDGE

Here you have a relatively large loop at the beginning of every other row. For garter stitch, scoop these loops up. Avoid this edging for stocking stitch!

Photo 10: Picking up stitches along the yo, k2togtbl edge

KNITTING THE FIRST ROW AFTER PICKING UP STITCHES

You can see from the photos that the stitches which have been picked up are mounted differently. Stitches picked up from a knitted edge and a s1p edge need to be knitted into the BACK of the stitch on the first row, while those picked up from a yo, k2togtbl edge need to be knitted normally.

SEWING SEAMS

There are times when you have to sew seams. The important thing to remember is LOOSE! You want a flat finish, and that is much easier to get if the pieces are flat to start with. Work on a table.

Photo 11: Sewing the knit edges

Make sure you use a tapestry needle of the right size for the yarn. Thin yarn, thin needle. But make sure it is blunt not sharp.

For shawls, the best seam is a simple 'over and over' whip stitch. Look at the size of the knitted stitches in your piece, and make your sewn ones the same size. This is usually much bigger and looser than when you are sewing up a sweater.

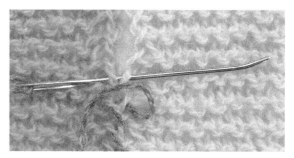

Photo 12: Sewing the S1p edges

Wherever possible, join row ends row for row. If you have used a s1p edge this is straightforward: pick up every chain along the edge, making sure you take the same leg each time.

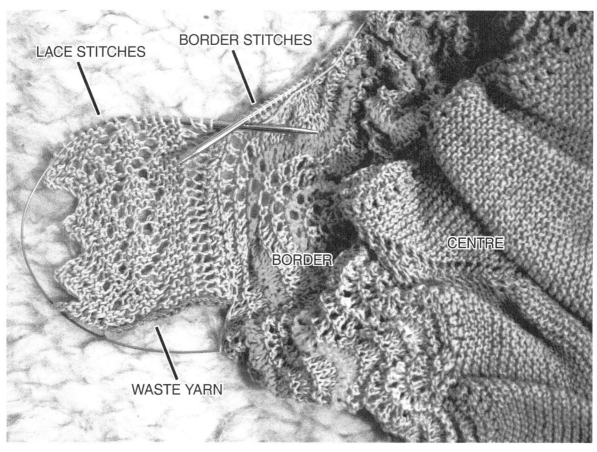

LACE STITCHES

BORDER STITCHES

BORDER

CENTRE

WASTE YARN

Photo 13: Knitting on the lace

If the row edges are all knit, they will consist of a 'knot' followed by a vertical strand. When sewing up take either the knot each time or the strand.

ADDING A LACE EDGING TO A KNITTED PIECE

It is quite possible to cast off stitches and then sew the edging neatly in place. If you would prefer to cast off at the same time as knitting the edging, this is how you do it. It is easier if these stitches are on a circular needle. I am going to call these the original stitches. You are also going to need a pair of straights of the same size.

Begin by casting on the lace edging stitches on the straights. If it is a shawl, you may want to cast on in a contrasting colour to graft the seam at the end. In this case, knit a couple of rows in the contrast before proceeding with the correct yarn. These stitches are your lace stitches (see Photo 13 on the previous page).

Now you are going to knit your lace and at the same time take in one of the original stitches at the end of the even numbered lace rows. To do this you knit the last stitch of the lace together with the next original stitch.

It is probably easiest to work with one straight needle and the circular containing the original stitches. In the photo I am working with one straight 6mm as before and one 6mm circ, both Addi brand. I have cast on the edging and knitted a couple of rows in turquoise yarn before starting the edging proper in purple yarn. I let the other end of the circ do its own thing.

The main problem with this technique is the first few rows. Once you have got the work established, it is very straightforward to work off the next 600 stitches!

GRAFTING OR KITCHENER STITCH

Once you know what you are doing this is straightforward, but the first couple of stitches are the problem. Make sure you pay attention to the exact size of the stitches you are making. Work on a table, not you knee, and never start any grafting of any type which you have a deadline ahead of you.

When stitches are grafted going in the same direction - for example the start and finish of a lace edging - it is possible to make the graft

Photo 14: Starting the graft

Photo 15: A few stitches grafted and removed from the needle

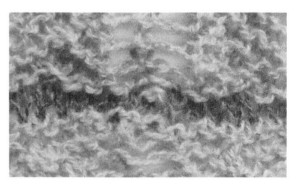
Photo 16: Result of graft (showing wrong side)

Photo 17: Result of graft (showing right side)

invisible. When the stitches are going in different directions - such as when grafting the two ends of a stole together - the loops are actually half a stitch out from each other, and it is impossible to form a totally imperceptible join. However, with very fine yarns and care, the join can be virtually impossible to see.

General Working Points

1. Make sure that your yarn and your needle have a really high contrast. If you have dark yarn, use light needles; if you have light yarn use dark needles.

2. Use needles with pointy tips. it doesn't matter what they are made of (wood for slow, polished metal for slick) but life will be much easier if the tips are sharp for poking through multiple stitches when decreasing.

3. Work in good light. Have the light behind you if possible, and if using artificial light, go for full spectrum bulbs (not daylight). These are much kinder to the eyes than any other sort.

4. Learn to read your knitting. Look at what you have just knitted. See the pattern of holes and lines of decreases. Compare it to the chart. If you do this after every couple of rows you will notice mistakes more easily, and be able to see where you are in the pattern if you loose your place.

5. Keep spare stitches on lengths of yarn, not on stitch holders. The ends of these can easily catch in the work and snag or break the yarn. Coilless pins, or a small plastic safety pins can be OK in the short term, but not if you put your work away!

> "START FINISHING BEFORE
> YOU START KNITTING"

BEFORE YOU START

1. Study the pattern in detail before you start knitting. Shetland patterns may look complex but they are made up of smaller motifs or patterns. Work these out before you put yarn to needle.

2. Work out reference points in your pattern. For example, know where you will have a

knit stitch right through the pattern, or where the yo on the current row will be one stitch over from that on the last row. These will help you to recognise mistakes very quickly so that you can put them right straight away rather than have lots of work to take back.

3. Swatching is extremely useful for several reasons. One, especially if it is a complicated lace pattern, it gives you a chance to learn it and understand it. Second, it gives you a chance to see if you will enjoy knitting a whole big creation using that pattern and that yarn. Finally, if you are designing your own thing - maybe putting together two different lace patterns, picking a lace pattern from the books around, designing your own lace pattern, or maybe just wanting to try something wildly different from anything you've tried before - you are going to have to swatch until you find what looks good to you.

4. Handle the washed, dried, dressed swatch because it might change size as it relaxes. Tug it, rumple it, leave it, then flatten it out and measure it, especially if the finished piece is going to a lively home.

5. Look at your swatch critically. have you used the best sized needles for that yarn and pattern? Some folk like their lace more dense than others. Work out what you like and stick with it.

In the examples I have used a different colour for seaming and grafting. Normally you would use the spare yarn at the start and finish of the piece. So make sure you leave enough yarn for the job. I routinely leave 24"/60 cm every time I start or finish a section.

WHEN KNITTING

1. Use stitch markers to your advantage. Exactly how many is a very personal thing, but if you are new to lace knitting, use a stitch marker between every few pattern repeats for a small pattern, or every repeat for a larger one. That way you can read your knitting more easily and see where you made your mistake.

2. Count your stitches often. That way you are more likely to pick up mistakes soon after they happen.

Photo 18: Dressing a Faroese mini shawl

3. Keep track of the row you are on. Use a row counter. If you are working in garter stitch, especially with fine yarns, it can be very easy to miss a row. Keep a note of which row of the chart you are working on either by putting a ruler ABOVE the current row (so you can see how the current row relates to the rows before) or using removable highlighter tape. Using a magnetic board and ruler also works well.

4. Use lifelines as often as you need. They only take a minute to put in and could save you having to take many rows back.

5. Enjoy your lace knitting. Don't make yourself do it if you are tired - that way leads to mistakes. Lace can be mentally relaxing, but have some other knitting on the needles for when you are really stressed and tired.

Dressing Your Shawl

This is drying the lace under tension, to open up the holes and define the points of a peaked edging. It takes a long time to dress a shawl properly - make sure you have a good hour set aside for the job.

You will need a flat surface, larger than your shawl, into which you can stick pins. This can be a special cork or foam board, or can be the carpet of the spare room. You will also need quilting pins - the type with a large head - or knitter's pins. You might need a ruler or tape measure.

Place the shawl on the surface, in the middle. Spread it out roughly at first, then start to smooth it to shape from the centre. You are aiming to flatten the shawl, and open up the

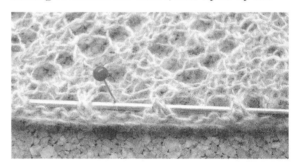

Photo 19: Detail of lace wires in use

holes. This means that you are going to be putting the knitting under tension. Don't pull too hard. If in doubt pull it less than you think; you can go back and tension it more later. You might find a tape measure or long rule useful in getting a perfect square or circle.

Once the shawl is getting towards the correct shape and size, start pinning. If the centre has holes round it, put in wires here. Remember you will probably have to take out these initial pins as the shaping continues. This is backbreaking work - don't hurry it!

If you have a peaked edging you will need to pin every single point. Start by pinning every fourth one until all the lace is pinned in this way. Then go round again pinning the points in between. Don't be too surprised if you find you have to re-pin complete sections.

If you are making circular shawls, then flexible wires make the job easier.

Once the shawl is pinned to your satisfaction leave it to dry. Wait until the shawl feels dry – then leave for another 24 hours before starting to remove the pins.

IF YOU DON'T HAVE BOARDS, IMPROVISE

If you have a spare wall, cork tiles attached to it makes an excellent dressing board. If you have a spare double bed, use that. Cover it with thick, fluffy towels. – the fluffy is important. Start from the centre, and smooth the shawl out over the towels; friction will hold it in place. Then pull out each scallop individually. If you need to use pins, make sure they are quilter's pins - long, with a prominent head - so that you are less likely to spear your next guest.

If you need to speed up the drying process, use a hair dryer! Don't hold it too close, and keep the stream of air moving, much as you would when drying your hair. Remember to continue

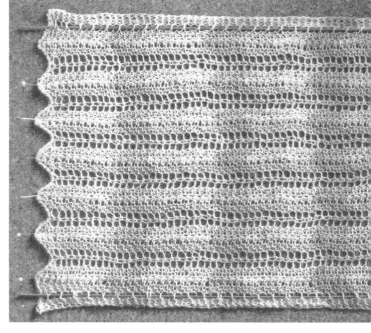

Photo 20: Pinning the peaks

for a while after the shawl feels dry, then leave it in the open for 24 hours afterwards for the moisture inside the fibre to evaporate.

And if you have neither space nor time, consider pressing. This works very well if you are careful and methodical. Put a thick towel on your ironing board, or on the table. Place the shawl on this and cover with a terry tea towel. Put the iron down on this for a few seconds. Work from the centre out, doing one border at a time. Finish with the lace edging, pulling the scallops as you press. (If you are nervous of this, try it out with your swatch first.)

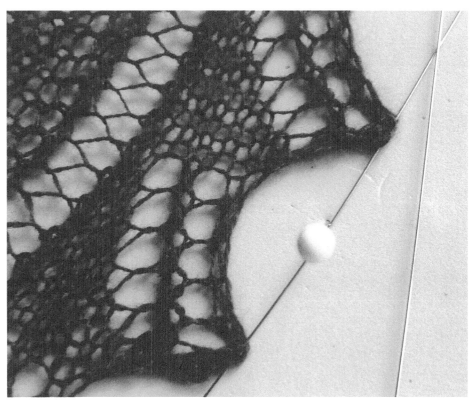

Photo 21: Flexible wires for dressing a circular shawl

Shawl Shape Families

Shape Families

There are three families - triangles, squares and circles. Other shapes are a combination of these, for example crescents are made up of a square and two triangles and a hexagon is made up of six triangles.

Triangles can be narrow or wide, shallow or deep.

Squares includes rectangles.

Circles includes semi-circles and ovals.

THE TRIANGLE FAMILY

Knitted triangles can be a variety of shapes, but they are usually variations of isosceles – i.e. they have two edges the same length. In addition, triangular shawls are often themselves made up of other triangles.

There are two possible ways to knit a triangle – point up or long side (hypotenuse) down. Variations of the point up are usually used (yarn overs increase stitch numbers easily) BUT this can look like top down.

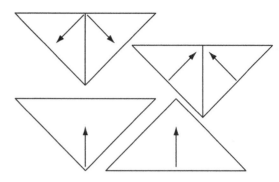

Diagram 1: Triangle construction possibilities

In Diagram 1, the upper left drawing shows a popular construction method. At first sight, it looks like top down, BUT the shawl is actually being made a TWO triangles from the POINT UP.

If the increases are at each end of every row, a wide triangle is formed, which was known in Victorian times as a fischou.

POINT UP

Here you start at the tip, and work upwards, the longest edge of the triangle being on the needle at any one time. Increases are made on or near each edge.

The rate of increase gives you the shape. With a garter stitch ground, the rate of 2 sts every other row gives you a right-angled triangle, with the right angle at the point. If you use this rate of increase for a stocking stitch piece you will get a narrower triangle.

HYPOTENUSE DOWN

This is where you work from the longest side towards the point. The decreases are made at the edges of the triangle. This might be at the two edges of the knitting, or the piece can be broken down into two or more sections, giving decreases within the rows.

BORDERS AND LACE

These can be added either as part of the main piece, or by knitting on later. If the latter, they can be done by picking up stitches and knitting down, or by knitting on sideways.

PATTERNS FOR TRIANGULAR MINI SHAWLS

THE CIRCLE FAMILY

Almost all circular pieces are worked from the centre out. Here the decision is how to increase.

Tiered Increases   Radial Increases

Diagram 2: Circle construction possibilities

RADIAL INCREASES

Here you divide the piece into different segments and increase at these points regularly throughout the shawl. This means that the stitch number increases every few rows.

If you are working with a stocking stitch ground, you will need to increase 6 stitches every other round. If you are working with a garter stitch ground, you will need to increase 7 or 8 stitches every other round. Those are the basic ratios. You can, however, alter them slightly. For example, often you will increase 12 stitches (six panels with two increases) every fourth round on a stocking stitch ground.

TIERED INCREASES

Here you increase a lot of stitches on a few rows, with large numbers of rows between. You effectively have a block with the same number of stitches, then an increase row, then another block with a larger number of stitches. The 'Pi' formula is one such system, but not the only one.

This method gives a series of concentric circles. Each ring has a set number of stitches, and continuous designs in that segment work well. The Pi formula can be used to make a shawl using this system. Here the design is based on the principle that if you double the number of stitches and double the number of

rows between increases, you will end up with a circular shawl.

BORDERS AND LACE

Whichever way you work your shawl, a border is worked as part of the design. The lace, if you have one, can be knitted straight down or sideways.

PATTERNS FOR CIRCULAR MINI SHAWLS

THE SQUARE FAMILY

The ways to knit squares are many and various, but the basically fall into two categories: centre out and outside in.

If you have a shawl with centre, border and edging, you can knit the centre square in several ways – centre out (basically 4 triangles); corner to corner, increasing then decreasing; or straight up from one edge.

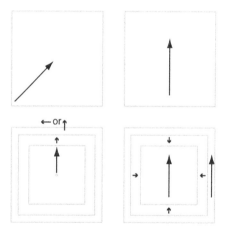

Diagram 3: Square construction possibilities

There are many different variations on these themes.

INSIDE OUT

Here the centre is knitted first, then the borders are picked up round the centre and worked outwards. The four borders may be knitted individually, with the mitres sewn later, or they may be knitted together in the round. The edging may also be knitted outwards, or may be knitted on side ways.

OUTSIDE IN

The lace edging is knitted first, either in one piece or four separate pieces. Stitches are then picked up along the straight edge, and the four border pieces are knitted on. The centre is then knitted from the final border. The live stitches from the completed centre are then grafted to the opposite border, and the side border stitches are sewn to the sides of the centre. Note that traditionally with fine shawls the side stitches were not knitted off as this forms too thick a ridge: instead, they were grafted.

PATTERNS FOR SQUARE MINI SHAWLS

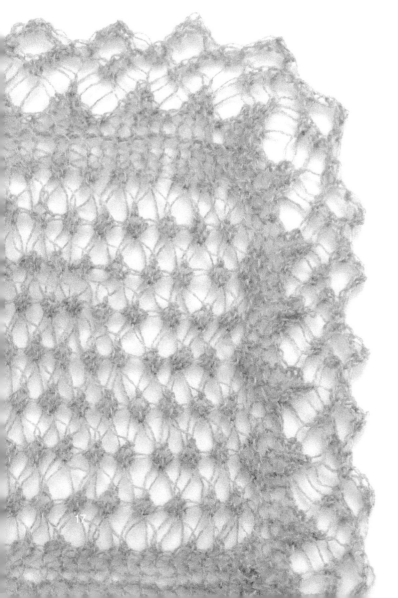

OTHER SHAPES

CRESCENTS

Over the past couple of years, the crescent shawl has become very popular. This is basically part of a very large circle, or of two triangles and square, and is a modification of the fischou. Crescents can be working in two ways: from end to end or by short rows.

Crescent shawls usually have a centre (often garter stitch) and a lace edging. They do not have a border. When worked from end to end the increases and decreases are placed between the centre and the lace. When

Diagram 4: Crescents

worked using short rows, the lace is worked first, and then the centre is worked up from the edge of the lace using short rows.

PATTERNS FOR CRESCENT MINI SHAWLS

FAROESE SHAWLS

Faroese shawls are made up of two triangles with a central gusset between them. The combined effect of this panel, plus the decreases within each triangular 'wing' of the shawl, makes Faroese shawls stay on the shoulders better than many flat shawls. The central gusset is an acute angled triangle with the top cut off!

PATTERNS FOR FAROESE SHAWLS

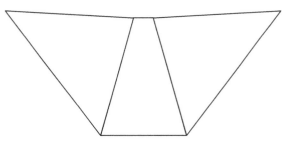

Diagram 5: Faroese

Let's start by getting the problems out of the way! First, there is no standard set of symbols – everyone has their own way of charting, and the same symbol can mean different things in different books. Second, if the yarn-over and its decrease do not come next to each other you can have a chart which does not look like the final knitted piece. This can be very confusing.

Once you realise these limitations, you will probably find that working from a chart allows you to see how you are progressing with a pattern, and to give you an early warning if something has gone wrong!

The Chart

Each square on the chart represents one action. (This is slightly different from texture or colourwork charts where every square represents one stitch.) Rows are worked from the bottom of the chart to the top. Stitches are numbered from the right to the left. Charts are read from the bottom up and right to left for odd numbered rows and left to right for even numbered rows.

The chart may have uneven edges, or spaces in the middle. This is due to differing numbers of stitches on different rows. The 'no stitch' spaces are arranged so that the charts reads well, and as nearly as possible, the yos are shown as the pattern of holes will be in the knitted piece.

The Symbols

An 'empty' square represents the ground stitch. In most cases in Shetland lace this will be a knit stitch on odd and even numbered rows, as Shetland lace is usually knitted on a garter stitch ground. If the pattern is on a stocking stitch ground, the empty square will be knit on odd numbered rows and purl on even numbered rows. Other actions are represented by different symbols. The symbols used in this book are on page 5. For example, ○ represents a yarn-over, and / represents a right leaning decrease (k2tog).

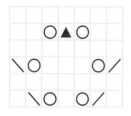

Cat's Paw Chart

Reading a chart

Let's take the example of the Cat's Paw. There are 7 squares across the bottom, which means you need 7 stitches.

Row 1 starts at the bottom right. The first square you come to is empty, so this is a knit stitch. The next is a right leaning decrease, k2tog, then a yarn-over, a knit stitch and another yarn-over. Now a left leaning decrease, so your choice of k2togtbl or ssk, and finally another knit stitch. And if this is written out as in a pattern it becomes k1, k2tog, yo, k1, yo, k2togtbl, k1.

Row 2 is read from left to right. It is all empty squares, so is all knit.

Row 3 becomes k2tog, yo, k3, yo, k2togtbl

Row 4 becomes all k

Row 5 starts with k2, yo, then k3togtbl, then yo, k2

Row 6 becomes all knit

WHEN THERE ARE SYMBOLS ON EVEN-NUMBERED ROWS

Even numbered rows are read from left to right. Actions like knit or yarn-over will be exactly the same as on odd numbered rows, but left and right leaning decreases will need different actions for the same effect. So the symbol / means k2tog on odd numbered rows, but k2togtbl on even numbered rows.

This concept can be tricky to get your head round. Personally, I think of myself looking round the back of the paper! From the front / is right leaning, with its head to the right side of the page, but when viewed from the other side of the paper it still has it head to the edge of the page, but now it is leaning to the left. I suggest you play with scrap paper and pencil!

If in doubt, go to the key for your chart. There it will tell you what action to perform on odd and even numbered rows.

If we look at the Vandyke Lace (next page) you see the chart is more complex that the Cat's

Paw. There are yarn-overs on every row, and there are extra symbols. In addition, one edge is jagged. But as before the trick is to read the chart one row at a time.

Row 1 is straightforward. k2, yo, ssk, yo, yo, k1. Note the two yarn-overs next to each other. Note that you use up 6 stitches (k2, ssk, ssk) but end up with 7 (3 yarn-overs, 2 decreases).

Row 2 starts with a yarn-over, then k2, then the dot, which the key will tell you means a purl stitch. Then k2, yo, ssk. The positioning of the chart puts the yarn-over at the start of the row over to the left, so that the stitches within the body of the piece line up.

Rows 3 and 4 are straightforward.

Row 5 has five yarn-overs but only three decreases, so you end up with two more stitches than you started with. Again, these are placed to the left so the stitches line up.

Row 9 is similar to Row 5, but with seven yarn-overs and four decreases. So the chart continues three squares over from the row before.

On Row 12, 7 stitches are cast off at the start of the row. This brings the left hand edge of the chart inwards by those 7 squares. Note that the stitch left on the receiving needle after the cast-offs is the first of the 4 knit stitches before the yarn-over, ssk.

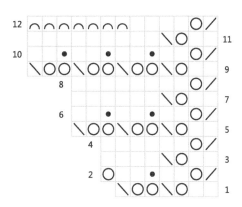

Vandyke Chart

Charting Odd Numbered Rows Only

If there are no yarn-overs on even numbered rows, these may not be charted. You MUST look at the instructions for each individual chart to see whether even numbered rows are charted, and if not, how to work them.

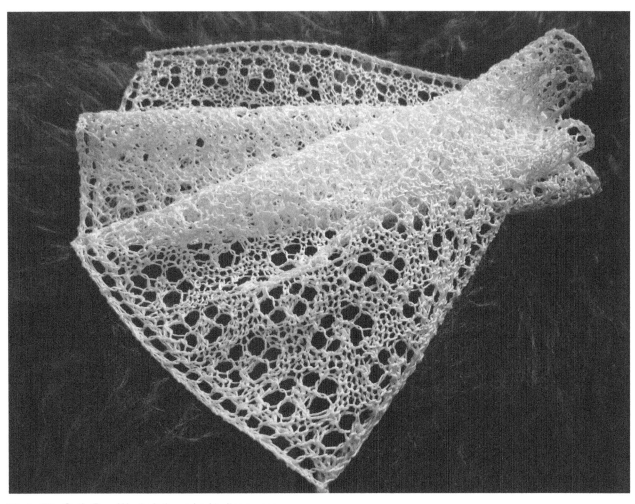

Photo 22: Cat's Paw Washcloth worked in linen yarn

Triangle Family

Tip-Up Triangular Shawl
Page 22

Mini Fischou
Page 27

Triangular Shawl with
Border & Lace
Page 23

End-to-End Crescent
Shawl
Page 28

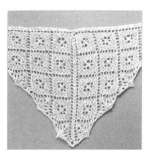

Two Tip-Up Triangles
Shawl
Page 25

Short-Row Crescent
Shawl
Page 29

Tip Up Triangular shawl

MATERIALS

About 8 g / 64 yds lace weight yarn

Pair 4 mm (US 6) needles

The original uses lace weight hand-spun; 100% Shetland wool; 800 yds per 100 g

SIZE

46 cm / 18" wide by 18 cm / 7" deep

TENSION

18 sts and 32 rows to 10 cm / 4" over pattern

CONSTRUCTION

The shawl is worked from the tip up.

Pattern

Cast on 3 sts. Work through the chart, repeating Rows 25 to 38 as desired.

Repeat Rows 37 and 38 once more. Cast off.

FINISHING

Weave in all ends. Wash and dress.

Tip-up Triangular shawl Chart

*Note that ODD numbered rows only are charted.
Even-numbered rows are worked as S1p, k to end of row.*

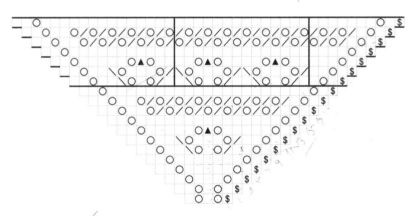

Row 1: S1p, k1, [yo, k1] twice.

Row 2 and all alternate rows: S1p, k to end of row.

Row 3: S1p, k1, [yo, k1] twice, k1.

Row 5: S1p, k1, yo, k3, yo, k2.

Row 7: S1p, k1, yo, k5, yo, k2.

Row 9: S1p, k1, yo, k7, yo, k2.

Row 11: S1p, k1, yo, k2, k2tog, yo, k, yo, ssk, k2, yo, k2.

Row 13: S1p, k1, yo, k2, k2tog, yo, k3, yo, ssk k2, yo, k2.

Row 15: S1p, k1, yo, k5, yo, k3togtbl, yo, k5, yo, k2.

Row 17: S1p, k1, yo, k15, yo, k2.

Row 19: S1p, k1, yo, k1, [k2tog, yo] to last 4 sts, k2, yo, k2.

Row 21: As Row 19.

Row 23: S1p, k1, yo, k to last 2 sts, yo, k2.

Row 25: S1p, k1, yo, [k2, k2tog, yo, k, yo, ssk] to last 4 sts, k2, yo, k2.

Row 27: S1p, k1, yo, k2, [k2tog, yo, k3, yo, ssk] to last 4 sts, k2, yo, k2.

Row 29: S1p, k1, yo, k5, [yo, k3togtbl, yo, k4] to last 3 sts, k1, yo, k2.

Row 31: As Row 23.

Rows 33 and 35: As Row 19.

Row 37: As Row 23.

Row 38: As Row 2.

Rows 25 to 38 form the pattern. Repeat them as required.

Triangular Shawl with Border & Lace

MATERIALS

25 g / 125 yds 4 ply (fingering) weight yarn

Pair 3.5 mm (US 4) needles

Thin needle for picking up stitches

1 stitch marker

Waste yarn

The original uses J&S 2 ply jumper weight; 100% Shetland wool; 125 yds per 25 g

SIZE

66 cm / 26" by 36 cm / 14"

TENSION

16 sts and 22 rows to 10 cm / 4" over centre pattern

CONSTRUCTION

The centre triangle is worked first from the tip up. The loops from the row ends are picked up and the borders are worked. The lace edging is then worked all round the shawl.

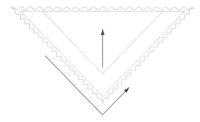

Pattern

CENTRE

Cast on 3 sts.

Row 1: K1, yo, k1 yo, k1.

Row 2: S1p, k to end of row.

Work from the chart, repeating Rows 23 to 34 until there are 75 sts on the needle.

Do not break yarn. Leave these 75 sts on waste yarn.

BORDER

With RS facing and using the thin needle, pick up 37 sts down one side of the triangle, PM, pick up 37 sts up the other side. 74 sts.

Using the main needles and the yarn from the centre, knit one row.

Now work from the Border Chart, placing it twice on each row as follows:

Row 1: Work through Row 1 of the chart, SM, work Row 1 of the chart.

Row 2: K.

Continuing in this manner, work through the Border Chart. 126 sts

Do not break the yarn. Leave the sts on the needle.

LACE EDGING

With waste yarn, cast on 5 sts.

Change to the working yarn and work from the Lace Chart, noting that for every repeat of the chart (20 rows) you remove 10 sts from the border.

Work through the Lace Chart six times. 3 sts remain before the marker. Now work the Lace Corner Chart, noting that this will remove the 3 sts before the marker and 3 sts after. Work through the Lace Chart six times more. All the border sts have been removed.

THE TOP EDGE

With right side facing, pick up 12 sts from the edge of the left border, place the 75 sts from the top of the Centre on the needle, then pick up 13 sts from the edge of the right border. 100 sts.

Work through the Lace Chart ten times. Break yarn leaving a long tail for grafting.

FINISHING

Remove the waste yarn from the start of the lace. Graft the stitches from the start and end of the lace together. Weave in all ends. Wash and dress.

CENTER CHART

Note that ODD ROWS ONLY are charted. Work even-numbered rows as S1p, k to end of row.

Row 1: S1p, k1, yo, k1, yo, k2.

Row 2 and all alternate rows: S1p, k to end of row.

Row 3: S1p, k1, yo, k3, yo, k2.

Row 5: S1p, k1, yo, k5, yo, k2.

Row 7: S1p, k1, yo, k7, yo, k2.

Row 9: S1p, k1, yo, k9, yo, k2.

Row 11: S1p, k1, yo, k11, yo, k2.

Row 13: S1p, k1, yo, k5, yo, k3togtbl, yo, k5, yo, k2.

Row 15: S1p, k1, yo, k4, yo, k3togtbl, yo, k1, yo, k3togtbl, yo, k4, yo, k2.

Row 17: S1p, k1, yo, k7, yo, k3togtbl, yo, k7, yo, k2.

Row 19: S1p, k1, yo, k19, yo, k2.

Row 21: S1p, k1, yo, k21, yo, k2.

Row 23: S1p, k1, yo, k to last 2 sts, yo, k2.

Row 25: S1p, k1, yo, k3, *k2, yo, k3togtbl, yo, k7. Repeat from * to last 12 sts, k2, yo, k3togtbl, yo, k5, yo, k2.

Row 27: S1p, k1, yo, k4, *yo, k3togtbl, yo, k1, yo, k3togtbl, yo, k5. Repeat from * to last 13 sts, yo, k3togtbl, yo, k1, yo, k3togtbl, yo, k4, yo, k2.

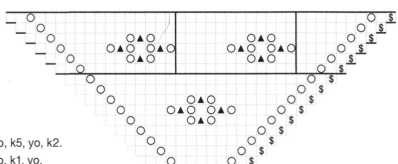

Row 29: S1p, k1, yo, k5, *k2, yo, k3togtbl, yo, k7. Repeat from * to last 14 sts, k2, yo, k3togtbl, yo, k7, yo, k2.

Row 31: As Row 23.

Row 33: As Row 23.

Row 34: S1p, k to end of row.

Rows 23 to 34 form the pattern. Repeat them as required.

BORDER CHART

Note that ODD ROWS ONLY are charted. On even-numbered rows, knit all stitches.

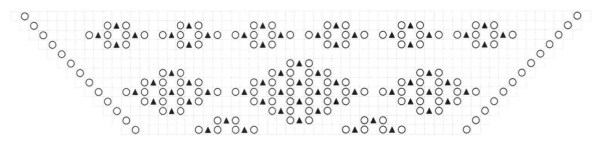

Row 1: K1, yo, k6, yo, k3togtbl, yo, k1, yo, k3togtbl, yo, k9, yo, k3togtbl. yo. k1, yo, k3togtbl, yo, k6, yo, k1.

Row 2 and all even numbered rows: K.

Row 3: K1, yo, k9, [yo, k3togtbl, yo, k5] twice, yo, k3togtbl, yo, k9, yo, k1.

Row 5: K1, yo, k4, yo, k3togtbl, yo, k9, yo, k3togtbl, yo, k1, yo, k3togtbl, yo, k9, yo, k3togtbl, yo, k4, yo, k1.

Row 7: K1, yo, k3, [yo, k3togtbl, yo, k1, yo, k3togtbl, yo, k5, yo, k3togtbl, yo, k1] twice, yo, k3togtbl, yo, k3, yo, k1.

Row 9: K1, yo, k2, [yo, k3togtbl, yo, k1] nine times, yo, k3togtbl, yo, k2, yo, k1.

Row 11: K1, yo, k5, [yo, k3togtbl, yo, k1, yo, k3togtbl, yo, k5, yo, k3togtbl, yo, k1] twice, yo, k3togtbl, yo, k5, yo, k1.

Row 13: K1, yo, k8, yo, k3togtbl, yo, k9, yo, k3togtbl, yo, k1, yo, k3togtbl, yo, k9, yo, k3togtbl, yo, k8, yo, k1.

Row 15: K1, yo, k23, yo, k3togtbl, yo, k23, yo, k1.

Row 17: K1, yo, k51, yo, k1.

Row 19: K1, [yo, k5, yo, k3togtbl] six times, yo, k5, yo, k1.

Row 21: K1, yo, k4, [yo, k3togtbl, yo, k1] eleven times, yo, k3togtbl, yo, k4, yo, k1.

Row 23: K1, yo, k7, [yo, k3togtbl, yo, k5] five times, yo, k3togtbl, yo, k7, yo, k1.

Row 25: K1, yo, k59, yo, k1.

Row 26: As Row 2.

Charts for the Triangular Shawl with Border & Lace continue on page 74.

Two Tip-Up Triangles Shawl

MATERIALS

30 g / 150 yds 4 ply (fingering) weight yarn

Pair 4.5 mm (US 7) needles

3 stitch markers

Waste yarn

The original uses J&S 2 ply jumper weight; 100% Shetland wool; 125 yds per 25 g

SIZE

36 cm / 14" by 71 cm / 28"

TENSION

14 sts and 20 rows to 10 cm / 4" over centre pattern

CONSTRUCTION

The shawl is knitted from the centre back down, as two, tip-up, triangles. The border is knitted straight on to the centre.

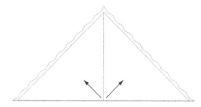

Pattern

CENTRE

With waste yarn, cast on 10 sts.

Foundation Row: K2, PM, k3, PM, k3, PM, k2.

You now have a 2 st border, two triangles of 3 sts each and another 2 st border.

Work from the chart, placing it twice in each row as follows:

Row 1: S1p, k1, SM, work from the chart, SM, work from the chart, SM, k2.

Row 2 and all alternate rows: S1p, k to end of row.

Work through the chart then work Rows 29 to 42 once more.

LOWER BORDER

Now work the Border Chart, placing it as before.

Cast off very loosely.

FINISHING

Remove the waste yarn and place 5 sts on each of two needles. Graft these stitches together to form a continuous garter stitch border along the top of the shawl.

Weave in all ends. Wash and dress.

CENTRE CHART

Note that ODD ROWS ONLY are charted. On even-numbered rows, knit all stitches.

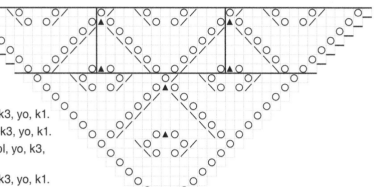

Row 1: [K, yo] twice, k1.

Row 2 and all alternate rows: K.

Row 3: K1, yo, k3, yo, k1.

Row 5: K1, yo, k5, yo, k1.

Row 7: K1, yo, k7, yo, k1.

Row 9: K1, yo, k9, yo, k1.

Row 11: K1, yo, k3, k2tog, yo, k1, yo, ssk, k3, yo, k1.

Row 13: K1, yo, k3, k2tog, yo, k3, yo, ssk, k3, yo, k1.

Row 15: [K1, yo] twice, ssk, k3, yo, k3togtbl, yo, k3, k2tog, [yo, k1] twice.

Row 17: K1, yo, k3, yo, ssk, k7, k2tog, yo, k3, yo, k1.

Row 19: K1, yo, k5, yo, ssk, k5, k2tog, yo, k5, yo, k1.

Row 21: K1, yo, k7, yo, ssk, k3, k2tog, yo, k7, yo, k1.

Row 23: K1, yo, k9, yo, ssk, k1, k2tog, yo, k9, yo, k1.

Row 25: K1, yo, k3, k2tog, yo, k1, yo, ssk, k3, yo, k3togtbl, yo, k3, k2tog, yo, k1, yo, ssk, k3, yo, k1.

Row 27: K1, yo, k3, k2tog, yo, k3, yo, ssk, k2, k2tog, yo, k3, k2tog, yo, k3, yo, ssk, k3, yo, k1.

Row 29: [K1, yo] twice, ssk, k3, yo, k3togtbl, *yo, k3, k2tog, yo, k1, yo, ssk, k3, yo, k3togtbl. Repeat from * to last 7 sts, yo, k3, k2tog, [yo, k1] twice.

Row 31: K1, yo, k3, yo, ssk, k4, *k3, k2tog, yo, k3, yo, ssk, k4. Repeat from * to last 9 sts, k3, k2tog, yo, k3, yo, k1.

Row 33: K1, yo, k5, yo, ssk, k3, *k2, k2tog, yo, k5, yo, ssk, k3. Repeat from * to last 10 sts, k2, k2tog, yo, k5, yo, k1.

Row 35: K1, yo, k7, yo, ssk, k2, *k1, k2tog, yo, k7, yo, ssk, k2. Repeat from * to last 11 sts, k1, k2tog, yo, k7, yo, k1.

Row 37: K1, yo, k9, yo, ssk, k1, *k2tog, yo, k9, yo, ssk, k1. Repeat from * to last 12 sts, k2tog, yo, k9, yo, k1.

Row 39: K1, *yo, k3, k2tog, yo, k1, yo, ssk, k3, yo, k3togtbl. Repeat from * to last 12 sts, yo, k3, k2tog, yo, k1, yo, ssk, k3, yo, k1.

Row 41: K1, yo, *k3, k2tog, yo, k3, yo, ssk, k2, k2tog, yo. Repeat from * to last 14 sts, k3, k2tog, yo, k3, yo, ssk, k3, yo, k1.

Row 42: K.

Rows 29 to 42 form the pattern. Repeat them as necessary.

LOWER BORDER CHART

*Note that **ODD ROWS ONLY** are charted. On even-numbered rows, knit all stitches.*

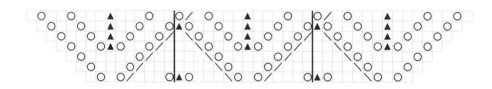

Row 1: K1, yo, k1, yo, ssk, k3, yo, k3togtbl, *yo, k3, k2tog, yo, k1, yo, ssk, k3, yo, k3togtbl. Repeat from * to last 7 sts, yo, k3, k2tog, yo, k1, yo, k1.

Row 2 and all alternate rows: K.

Row 3: K1, yo, k3, yo, ssk, k4, *k3, k2tog, yo, k3, yo, ssk, k4. Repeat from * to last 9 sts, k3, k2tog, yo, k3, yo, k1.

Row 5: K1, yo, k5, yo, ssk, k3, *k2, k2tog, yo, k5, yo, ssk, k3. Repeat from * to last 10 sts, k2, k2tog, yo, k5, yo, k1.

Row 7: K1, *yo, k2, yo, k3togtbl, yo, k2, yo, ssk, k3, k2tog. Repeat from * to last 8 sts, yo, k2, yo, k3togtbl, yo, k2, yo, k1.

Row 9: K1, *yo, k2, yo, k1, k3togtbl, k1, yo, k2, yo, ssk, K1, k2tog. Repeat from * to last 10 sts, yo, k2, yo, k1, k3togtbl, k1, yo, k2, yo, k1.

Row 11: K1, *[yo, k2] twice, k3togtbl, [k2, yo] twice, k3togtbl. Repeat from * to last 12 sts, [yo, k2] twice, k3togtbl, [k2, yo] twice, k1.

Row 13: K1, *yo, k2, yo, k3, k3togtbl, k3, yo, K1, k2tog. Repeat from * to last 14 sts, yo, k2, yo, k3, k3togtbl, k3, yo, k2, yo, k1.

Row 14: K.

Mini Fischou

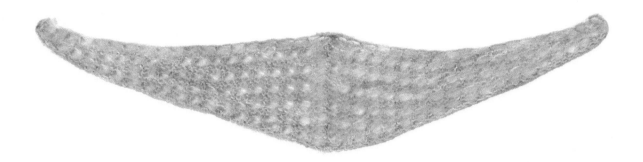

MATERIALS

4 g / 36 yds lace weight yarn

Pair 3.5 mm (US 5) needles

One 4 mm (US 6) needle for casting off

1 stitch marker

The original uses Manos Lace; 75% Baby alpaca / 20% Silk / 5% Cashmere; 439 yds per 50 g

SIZE

46 cm / 18" by 8 cm / 3"

TENSION

24 sts and 48 rows to 10 cm / 4" over pattern

CONSTRUCTION

The fischou is worked in one piece from the tip up.

Pattern

With 3.5 mm needles and lace weight yarn, cast on 5 sts and knit one row.

Now work from the chart until there are 77 sts on the needle.

Next Row: S1p, k1, yo, [k2tog, yo] to 1 st before M, k1, SM, yo, k3togtbl, yo, k1, [yo, ssk] to last 2 sts, yo, k2.

Next Row: S1p, k1, yo, k to last 2 sts, yo, k2.

Cast off using the larger needle.

FINISHING

Weave in all ends. Wash and dress.

Mini Fischou Chart

Note that ALL ROWS are charted.
A larger version of the chart only appears on page 81.

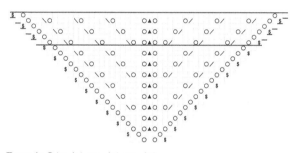

Row 1: S1p, k1, yo, k1, yo, k2.

Row 2 and all alternate rows: S1p, k1, yo, k to last 2 sts, yo, k2.

Row 3: S1p, k1, yo, k1, PM, yo, k3togtbl, yo, k1, yo, k2.

Row 5: S1p, k1, yo, k3, yo, k3togtbl, yo, k3, yo, k2.

Row 7: S1p, k1, yo, k2, k2tog, yo, k1, yo, k3togtbl, yo, k1, yo, ssk, k2, yo, k2.

Row 9: S1p, k1, yo, k2, k2tog, yo, k3, yo, k3togtbl, yo, k3, yo, ssk, k2, yo, k2.

Row 11: S1p, k1, yo, k2, k2tog, yo, k5, yo, k3togtbl, yo, k5, yo, ssk, k2, yo, k2.

Row 13: S1p, k1, yo, k2, k2tog, yo, k4, k2tog, yo, k1, yo, k3togtbl, yo, k1, yo, ssk, k4, yo, ssk, k2, yo, k2.

Row 15: S1p, k1, yo, k2, k2tog, yo, k4, k2tog, yo, k3, yo, k3togtbl, yo, k3, yo, ssk, k4, yo, ssk, k2, yo, k2.

Row 17: S1p, k1, yo, k2, k2tog, yo, k4, k2tog, yo, k5, yo, k3togtbl, yo, k5, yo, ssk, k4, yo, ssk, k2, yo, k2.

Row 19: S1p, k1, yo, k2, k2tog, yo, [k4, k2tog, yo] to 1 st before M, k1, SM, yo, k3togtbl, yo, k1, [yo, ssk, k4] to last 6 sts, yo, ssk, k2, yo, k2.

Row 21: S1p, k1, yo, k2, k2tog, yo, [k4, k2tog, yo] to 3 st before M, k3, SM, yo, k3togtbl, yo, k3, [yo, ssk, k4] to last 6 sts, yo, ssk, k2, yo, k2.

Row 23: S1p, k1, yo, k2, k2tog, yo, [k4, k2tog, yo] to 5 st before M, k5, SM, yo, k3togtbl, yo, k5, [yo, ssk, k4] to last 6 sts, yo, ssk, k2, yo, k2.

Row 24: As Row 2.

Repeat Rows 19 to 24 as required.

End-to-End Crescent Shawl

MATERIALS

20 g / 60 yds DK yarn

Pair 6 mm (US 10) needles

1 Stitch marker

The original uses Manos Silk Blend; 30% Silk, 70% Merino; 300 yds per 100g.

SIZE

71 cm / 28" by 13 cm / 5"

TENSION

20 sts by 20 rows to 10 cm / 4" over garter stitch

CONSTRUCTION

The shawl is started at one end, increased to the desired width, worked straight for the desired length, then decreased.

Pattern

Cast on 3 sts.

Row 1: K1, m1, k2.

Row 2: S1p, k to end of row.

Row 3: K1, m1, k3.

Row 4: S1p, k1, PM, k3.

Work from the Increase Chart, repeating Rows 11 to 18 until there are 22 sts on the needle (16 sts to the right of the marker).

Work through the Centre Chart 4 times, then work from the Decrease Chart until 5 sts remain.

Next Row: S1p, k3togtbl, k1.

Next Row: S1p, k2.

Next Row: K3togtbl.

Break yarn and draw through remaining stitch.

FINISHING

Weave in all ends. Wash and dress.

End-to-End Cresent Shawl Charts

INCREASE CHART

Note that ODD ROWS ONLY are charted. Even-numbered rows are worked as S1p, k to end of row.

Row 1: S1p, k1, yo, k1, SM, k2.

Row 2 and all alternate rows: S1p, k to end of row.

Row 3: S1p, k3, yo, k2.

Row 5: S1p, [k2, yo] twice, k2.

Row 7: S1p, k6, yo, k2.

Row 9: S1p, k3, yo, k4, yo, k2.

Row 11: S1p, k to M, k1, k2tog, yo, k, yo, k2.

Row 13: S1p, k to 1 st before M, yo, k1, SM, [k2tog, yo] twice, k1, yo, k2.

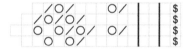

Row 15: S1p, k to M, k1, [k2tog, yo] twice, k2tog, k1.

Row 17: S1p, k to 1 st before M, yo, k1, SM, k2, k2tog, yo, k2tog, k1.

Row 18: As Row 2.

CENTRE CHART

Note that ODD ROWS ONLY are charted. Even-numbered rows are worked as S1p, k14.

Row 1: S1p, k to M, SM, k1, k2tog, yo, k1, yo, k2.

Row 2 and all alternate rows: S1p, k14.

Row 3: S1p, k to 3 st before M, k2tog, yo, k1, SM, (k2tog, yo) twice, k1, yo, k2.

Row 5: S1p, k to M, SM, k1, (k2tog, yo) twice, k2tog, k1.

Row 7: S1p, k to 3 sts before M, k2tog, yo, k1, SM, k2, k2tog, yo, k2tog, k1.

Row 8: As Row 2.

DECREASE CHART

Note that ODD rows only are charted. Even-numbered rows are worked as S1p, k to end of row.

Row 1: S1p, k to M, SM, k1, k2tog, yo, k1, yo, k2.

Row 2 and all alternate rows: S1p, k to end of row.

Row 3: S1p, k to 4 st before M, k3togtbl, yo, k1, SM, [k2tog, yo] twice, k1, yo, k2.

Row 5: S1p, k to M, SM, k1, [k2tog, yo] twice, k2tog, k1.

Row 7: S1p, k to 4 sts before M, k3togtbl, yo, k1, SM, k2, k2tog, yo, k2tog, k1.

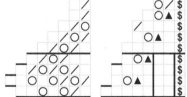

Charts instructions for the End-to-End Crescent Shawl continue on page 74.

Short-Row Crescent Shawl

MATERIALS

6 g / 86 yds cobweb weight yarn

Pair 3.5 mm (US 4) needles

Waste yarn

The original uses ColourMart 2/28; 100% Cashmere; 1400 yds per 100 g

SIZE

43 cm / 17" by 8 cm / 3"

TENSION

20 sts and 48 rows to 10 cm / 4" over garter stitch

CONSTRUCTION

The lace is knitted first, then the garter stitch centre, using short rows.

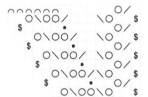

Short-Row Crescent Shawl Chart

Note that ALL ROWS are charted.

Row 1: S1p. k2, yo, ssk, yo, yo, ssk, yo, k2.

Row 2: S1p, k4, p1, k2, yo, ssk, k1.

Row 3: S1p, k2, yo, ssk, k2tog, yo, yo, ssk, yo, k2.

Row 4: S1p, k4, p1, k3, yo, ssk, k1.

Row 5: S1p, k2, yo, ssk, k1, k2tog, yo, yo, ssk, yo, k2.

Row 6: S1p, k4, p1, k4, yo, ssk, k1.

Row 7: S1p, k2, yo, ssk, k2, k2tog, yo, yo, ssk, yo, k2.

Row 8: S1p, k4, p1, k5, yo, ssk, k1.

Row 9: S1p, k2, yo, ssk, k3, k2tog, yo, yo, ssk, yo, k2.

Row 10: Cast off 6, k6, yo, ssk, k1.

Pattern

LACE

With waste yarn, cast on 9 sts.

Change to the working yarn, leaving a 3 yard tail for later, and knit 1 row.

Work through the Lace Chart 14 times. Break yarn leaving a short tail. Leave the sts on a thread.

CENTRE

Pick up 70 loops from the straight edge on to one needle. Now slip 25 of them on to the second needle, so that the tips of the two needles are together. The left hand needle has 45 sts on it and the right hand needle has 25 sts.

Rejoin yarn between needle tips and work as follows:

Row 1: K20, turn.

Row 2: K24, turn.

Row 3: K28, turn.

Row 4: K32, turn.

Continue in this way, adding 4 sts each time, until the row 'K68' has been worked.

Break yarn.

Slip the last stitch on to the full needle, then remove the waste yarn from the start of the lace and place those stitches on the needle. Using the tail from the start, knit all stitches, then pick up and knit the live stitches from the end of the lace.

Cast off all stitches loosely.

FINISHING

Weave in all ends. Wash and dress.

Square Family

Square Shawl from Four Triangles
Page 31

Square Shawl with Lace
Page 32

Stole with Lace
Page 33

Two-Tail Stole
Page 35

Diamond Shawl with Lace
Page 36

Square Shawl from Four Triangles

MATERIALS

18 g / 240 g cobweb weight yarn

Pair 3.5 mm (US 4) needles OR circular needle

3 OR 4 Stitch markers

Waste yarn

The original uses cobweb merino spun by Patricia Williams, New Zealand; 1320 m per 100 g

SIZE

38 cm / 15" square

TENSION

21 sts and 36 rows to 10 cm/ 4" over pattern

CONSTRUCTION

The shawl is worked from the centre out in rows. The seam is then sewn. Instructions are also given for converting the construction to working in the round.

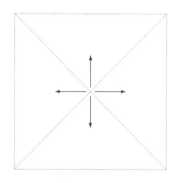

Pattern

Cast on 12 stitches into a ring.

Foundation Row: [K3, PM] three times, k3.

Work through the chart, noting that only odd numbered rows are charted, and that even numbered rows are all knit.

Repeat Rows 25 to 38 twice more.

EDGING

Row 1: *K1, yo, k to 1 st before M, yo, k1, SM. Repeat from * to end of row.

Row 2: K.

Row 3: K1, yo, *[k2tog, yo] to 2 sts before M, k1, yo, k1, SM. Repeat from * to end of round.

Pattern instructions for the Square Shawl from Four Triangles continue on page 74.

Square Shawl from Four Triangles Chart

Note that ODD ROWS ONLY are charted. On even-numbered rows, knit all stitches.

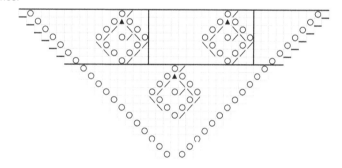

Row 1: [K1, yo] twice, k1.

Row 2 and all even numbered rows: K.

Row 3: K1, yo, k3, yo, k1.

Row 5: K1, yo, k5, yo, k1.

Row 7: K1, yo, k7, yo, k1.

Row 9: K1, yo, k9, yo, k1.

Row 11: K1, yo, k4, k2tog, yo, k5, yo, k1.

Row 13: K1, yo, k4, k2tog, yo, k1, yo, ssk, k4, yo, k1.

Row 15: K1, yo, k4, k2tog, yo, k3, yo, ssk, k4, yo, k1.

Row 17: K1, yo, k5, yo, ssk, k2tog, yo, k1, k2tog, yo, k5, yo, k1.

Row 19: K1, yo, k7, yo, ssk, k1, k2tog, yo, k7, yo, k1.

Row 21: K1, yo, k9, yo, k3togtbl, yo, k9, yo, k1.

Row 23: K1, yo, k10, k2tog, yo, k11, yo, k1.

Row 25: K1, yo, k2, *k2, k2tog, yo, k10. Repeat from * to last 10 sts, k2, k2tog, yo, k5, yo, k1.

Row 27: K1, yo, k3, *k1, k2tog, yo, k1, yo, ssk, k8. Repeat from * to last 11 sts, k1, k2tog, yo, k1, yo, ssk, k4, yo, k1.

Charts instructions for the Square Shawl from Four Triangles continue on page 74.

Square Shawl with Lace

MATERIALS

6g / 84 g cobweb weight yarn

Pair 3.75 mm (US 5) needles

3.75 mm (US 5) circular needle

Waste yarn

The original uses ColourMart 100% Cashmere 2.28; 1400 yds per 100 g

SIZE

23 cm / 9" square

TENSION

36 sts and 36 rows to 10 cm / 4" over centre pattern

CONSTRUCTION

The centre is worked from the bottom up. Stitches are picked up round the edge and the lace is knitted on sideways.

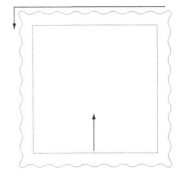

Pattern

CENTRE

With waste yarn, cast on 29 sts. Change to working yarn.

Row 1: S1p, k to end of row.

Repeat Row 1 three times more.

Work through the Centre Chart 14 times.

Repeat Row 1 four times. Do not break yarn.

Square Shawl with Lace Pattern Instructions continue on page 74; Charts and instructions are found on page 75.

Stole with Lace

MATERIALS

8 g / 104 yds cobweb weight yarn

Pair 2.75 mm (US 2) needles

2 stitch markers

Waste yarn

The original uses ColourMart 3/35 nm; 50% Silk, 50% Cotton; 1300 yds per 100 g

SIZE

23 cm / 9" by 33 cm / 13"

TENSION

30 sts and 44 rows over 10 cm / 4" over centre pattern

CONSTRUCTION

The bottom lace is knitted first, then the side laces and centre are knitted together. Finally the top lace is knitted, removing the centre stitches.

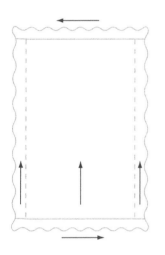

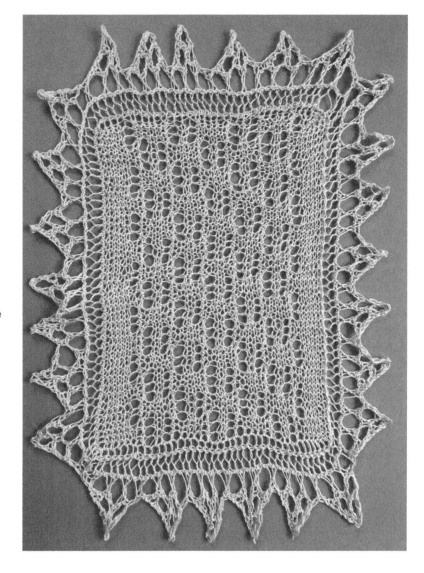

Pattern

BOTTOM LACE

With waste yarn cast on 7 sts. Change to main yarn and work through the 12 rows of the Bottom Lace Chart six times. Do not break yarn.

CENTRE AND SIDE LACE

Using the empty needle, and starting at the outer (scalloped) edge, remove the waste yarn from the start of the Bottom Lace, placing the 7 sts on the needle. Place marker. With the same needle, and starting from the same end, pick up 36 sts from the straight side of the Bottom Lace. Place marker. You

now have the 7 sts of the bottom lace on one needle, and the 36 sts of the centre plus the 7 sts from the start of the bottom lace on the other.

Complete the row as follows: SM, work the first row of the Centre Chart, SM, work the first row of the second side lace chart.

You now have both Side Laces and the Centre on the same needle, and are working all together.

Starting with the second row, continue working through the Centre Chart and the Side Lace Chart six times. Do not break yarn.

TOP EDGING

Work the Top Edging Chart through six times, noting that on each odd numbered row you knit the last stitch of the edging with the next stitch of the centre. Now work the 1st row of the chart again. 14 sts remain.

FINISHING

Graft the 7 sts of the left Side Lace with the 7 st of the Top Lace. Weave in all ends. Wash and dress the shawl, pinning out each scallop.

BOTTOM LACE

Note that ALL rows are charted

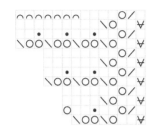

Row 1: S1p, k2, yo, ssk, yo, yo, ssk.

Row 2: Yo, k2, p1, k2, yo, ssk, k1.

Row 3: S1p, k2, yo, ssk, k4.

Row 4: K6, yo, ssk, k1.

Row 5: S1p, k2, yo, [ssk, yo, yo] twice, ssk.

Row 6: [K2, p1] twice, k2, yo, ssk, k1.

Row 7: S1p, k2, yo, ssk, k6.

Row 8: K8, yo, ssk, k1.

Row 9: S1p, k2, yo, [ssk, yo, yo] three times, ssk.

Row 10: [K2, p1] three times, k2, yo, ssk, k1.

Row 11: S1p, k2, yo, ssk, k9.

Row 12: Cast off 7, k4, yo, ssk, k1.

CENTRE

Note that ALL rows are charted

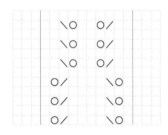

Row 1: K3, *k1, yo, ssk, k4, k2tog, yo, k1. Repeat from * to last 3 sts, k3.

Row 2 and all even numbered rows: K.

Row 3 and 5: As Row 1.

Row 7: K3, *k2, k2tog, yo, k2, yo, ssk, k2. Repeat from * to last 3 sts, k3.

Row 9 and 11: As Row 7.

Row 12: K.

SIDE LACES

Note that ALL rows are charted. The grey area in the chart represents the position of the Centre chart.

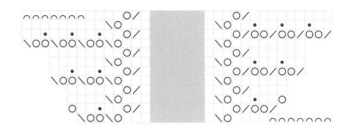

Row 1: Cast off 7, k4, yo, ssk, k1, work Centre Chart, k3, yo, ssk, yo, yo, ssk.

Row 2: Yo, k2, p1, k2, yo, ssk, k2, work Centre Chart, k3, yo, ssk, yo, yo, ssk.

Row 3: Yo, k2, p1, k2, yo, ssk, k1, work Centre Chart, k3, yo, ssk, k4.

Row 4: K6, yo, ssk, k1, work Centre Chart, k3, yo, ssk, k4.

Row 5: K6, yo, ssk, k1, work Centre Chart, k3, yo, [ssk, yo, yo] twice, ssk.

Row 6: [K2, p1] twice, k2, yo, ssk, k1, work Centre Chart, k3, yo, [ssk, yo, yo] twice, ssk.

Row 7: [K2, p1] twice, k2, yo, ssk, k1, work Centre Chart, k3, yo, ssk, k6.

Row 8: K8, yo, ssk, k1, work Centre Chart, k3, yo, ssk, k6.

Row 9: K8, yo, ssk, k1, work Centre Chart, k3, yo, [ssk, yo, yo] three times, ssk.

Row 10: [K2, p1] three times, k2, yo, ssk, k1, work Centre Chart, k3, yo, [k2tog, yo, yo] three times, ssk.

Row 11: [K2, p1] three times, k2, yo, ssk, k1, work Centre Chart, k3, yo, ssk, k9.

Row 12: Cast off 7, k4, yo, ssk, k1, work Centre Chart, k3, yo, ssk, k9.

TOP LACE

Note that ALL rows are charted

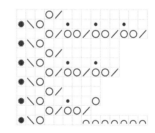

Row 1: Cast off 7, k4, yo, ssk, ktb.

Row 2: K3, yo, ssk, yo, yo, ssk.

Row 3: Yo, k2, p1, k2, yo, ssk, ktb.

Row 4: K3, yo, ssk, k4.

Row 5: K6, yo, ssk, ktb.

Row 6: K3, yo, [ssk, yo, yo] twice, ssk.

Row 7: [K2, p1] twice, k2, yo, ssk, ktb.

Row 8: K3, yo, ssk, k6.

Row 9: K8, yo, ssk, ktb.

Row 10: K3, yo, [ssk, yo, yo] three times, ssk.

Row 11: [K2, p1] three times, k2, yo, ssk, ktb.

Row 12: K3, yo, ssk, k9.

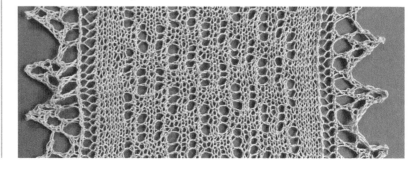

MATERIALS

20 g / 80 yds 4 ply (fingering) weight yarn

Pair 4.5 mm (US 7) needles

Stitch holder or waste yarn

The original uses 4 ply sock yarn; 75% Wool, 25% Nylon; 400 yds per 100 g

SIZE

17 cm / 8.5" by 51 cm / 20"

TENSION

22 sts and 24 rows to 10 cm / 4" over pattern

CONSTRUCTION

Each tail is worked separately then the live stitches are grafted in the centre.

Pattern

FIRST TAIL

Cast on 45 sts and knit 4 rows.

Work from the chart until tail measures about 8" or desired length, then work Row 1 again. Break yarn.

SECOND TAIL

Work as for the first tail. Break yarn leaving a enough yarn for grafting.

FINISHING

Graft the two tails together. Weave in all ends. Wash and dress.

Two-Tail Stole Chart

Note that ALL rows are charted.

Row 1: S1p, k2, *yo, k3, k3togtbl, k3, yo, k1. Repeat from * to last 2 sts, k2.

Row 2: S1p, k to end of row.

These two rows form the pattern. Repeat them as required.

Diamond Shawl with Lace

MATERIALS

38 g / 138 yds 4 ply (fingering) yarn

Pair 4 mm (US 6) needles

4 mm (US 6) circular needle

Waste yarn

The original uses Paton's 4 ply Cotton; 361 yds per 100 g

SIZE

33 cm / 13" square

TENSION

20 sts and 40 rows to 10 cm / 4" over centre pattern

CONSTRUCTION

The centre is worked first, from corner to corner. Stitches are picked up round the edge, and the lace is then knitted on sideways.

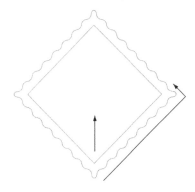

Pattern

CENTRE

Cast on 3 sts. Work through the chart noting that only odd numbered rows are charted. Even numbered rows are all worked S1p, k to end of row.

2 sts remain at end of chart. Do not break yarn.

LACE

Put the 2 remaining sts on the circular needle. Pick up 29 sts from one side of the centre, 29 sts from

Diamond Shawl with Lace Pattern Instructions continue on page 75.

CENTRE CHART

Note that ODD rows only are charted.
Even-numbered rows are worked as
S1p, k to end of row.

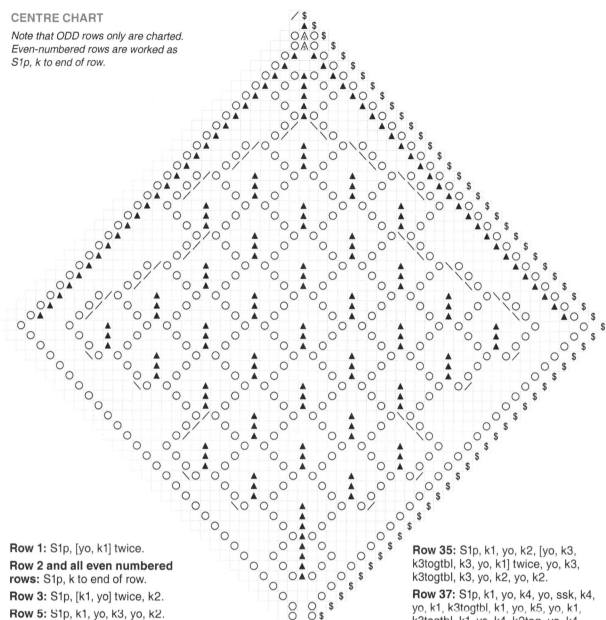

Row 1: S1p, [yo, k1] twice.

Row 2 and all even numbered rows: S1p, k to end of row.

Row 3: S1p, [k1, yo] twice, k2.

Row 5: S1p, k1, yo, k3, yo, k2.

Row 7: S1p, k1, yo, k5, yo, k2.

Row 9: S1p, k1, yo, k2, yo, k3togtbl, [yo, k2] twice.

Row 11: S1p, k1, yo, k2, yo, k1, k3togtbl, k1, yo, k2, yo, k2.

Row 13: S1p, k1, [yo, k2] twice, k3togtbl, [k2, yo] twice, k2.

Row 15: S1p, k1, yo, k4, yo, k1, k3togtbl, k1, yo, k4, yo, k2.

Row 17: S1p, k1, yo, k6, yo, k3togtbl, yo, k6, yo, k2.

Row 19: S1p, k1, yo, k6, yo, k1, k3togtbl, k1, yo, k6, yo, k2.

Row 21: S1p, k1, yo, k6, yo, k2, k3togtbl, k2, yo, k6, yo, k2.

Row 23: S1p, k1, yo, k3, k2tog, yo, k1, yo, k3, k3togtbl, k3, yo, k1, yo,

ssk, k3, yo, k2.

Row 25: S1p, k1, yo, k4, yo, k1, k3togtbl, k1, yo, k5, yo, k1, k3togtbl, k1, yo, k4, yo, k2.

Row 27: S1p, k1, yo, k4, yo, k2, k3togtbl, k2, yo, k3, yo, k2, k3togtbl, k2, yo, k4, yo, k2.

Row 29: S1p, k1, yo, k1, k2tog, [yo, k1, yo, k3, k3togtbl, k3] twice, yo, k1, yo, ssk, k1, yo, k2.

Row 31: S1p, k1, yo, k2, [yo, k1, k3togtbl, k1, yo, k5] twice, yo, k1, k3togtbl, k1, yo, k2, yo, k2.

Row 33: S1p, k, yo, k2, [yo, k2, k3togtbl, k2, yo, k3] twice, yo, k2, k3togtbl, [k2, yo] twice, k2.

Row 35: S1p, k1, yo, k2, [yo, k3, k3togtbl, k3, yo, k1] twice, yo, k3, k3togtbl, k3, yo, k2, yo, k2.

Row 37: S1p, k1, yo, k4, yo, ssk, k4, yo, k1, k3togtbl, k1, yo, k5, yo, k1, k3togtbl, k1, yo, k4, k2tog, yo, k4, yo, k2.

Row 39: S1p, k1, yo, k6, yo, ssk, k2, yo, k2, k3togtbl, k2, yo, k3, yo, k2, k3togtbl, k2, yo, k2, k2tog, yo, k6, yo, k2.

Row 41: S1p, k1, yo, k8, yo, ssk, yo, k3, k3togtbl, k3, yo, k1, yo, k3, k3togtbl, k3, yo, k2tog, yo, k8, yo, k2.

Row 43: S1p, k1, yo, k8, [yo, k1, k3togtbl, k1, yo, k5] twice, yo, k1, k3togtbl, k1, yo, k8, yo, k2.

Row 45: S1p, k1, yo, k8, [yo, k2, k3togtbl, k2, yo, k3] twice, yo, k2,

Diamond Shawl with Lace Charts and Chart Instructions continue on page 75.

37

Circle Family

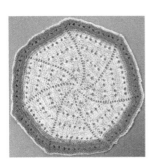

Spiral Shawl
Page 39

Wedge Circular Shawl
Page 41

Pi Mini Shawl
Page 43

Semi-Circular Shawl
Page 44

Spiral Shawl

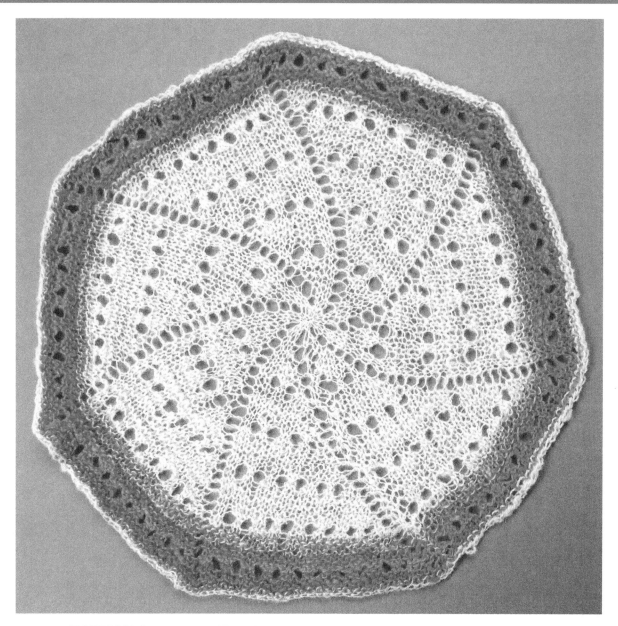

MATERIALS

6 g / 80 yds of cobweb weight yarn

Pair 2.75 mm (US 2) needles

OR

105 yds of chunky yarn

Pair 9 mm (US 13) needles

6 or 7 stitch markers

Waste yarn

The originals use 2 ply cobweb handspun; 100% Australian merino yarn; 1200 yds per 100 g and thick-and-thin chunky yarn made from a batt of merino/bamboo/alpaca/mohair; 150 yds per 100 g.

The cobweb shawl is worked to and fro, and the chunky shawl is worked in the round in stocking stitch.

SIZE

Cobweb shawl 22 cm / 9" in diameter; chunky shawl 60 cm / 24" in diameter

TENSION

30 sts and 48 rows to 10 cm / 4" over garter stitch cobweb pattern

8 sts and 12 rows to 10 cm / 4" over stocking stitch chunky pattern

CONSTRUCTION

The shawl is worked from the centre out, either to and fro or in the round.

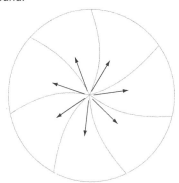

Pattern

FOR WORKING TO AND FRO IN GARTER STITCH

Cast on 7 sts.

SET UP

Row 1: Kfb seven times. 14 sts

Row 2: [K2, PM] to end of row.

Now work through the chart, placing it seven times on each row between markers.

Cast off loosely.

FINISHING

Sew up seam. Weave in ends. Wash and dress flat, pulling into shape either as a circle, hexagon or star.

FOR WORKING IN THE ROUND IN STOCKING STITCH

Cast on 6 sts into a ring.

SET UP

Round 1: Kfb six times. 12 sts

Round 2: [K2, PM] six times.

Now work through the chart, placing it six times on each row between markers.

Cast off purl-wise.

FINISHING

Weave in all ends. Wash and dress, pulling into shape either as a circle, hexagon or star.

FOR WORKING TO AND FRO IN GARTER STITCH

Note that ODD ROWS ONLY are charted. On even-numbered rows, knit all stitches.

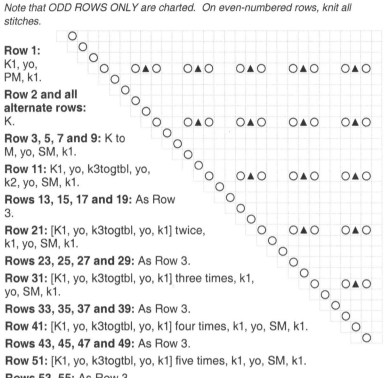

Row 1: K1, yo, PM, k1.

Row 2 and all alternate rows: K.

Row 3, 5, 7 and 9: K to M, yo, SM, k1.

Row 11: K1, yo, k3togtbl, yo, k2, yo, SM, k1.

Rows 13, 15, 17 and 19: As Row 3.

Row 21: [K1, yo, k3togtbl, yo, k1] twice, k1, yo, SM, k1.

Rows 23, 25, 27 and 29: As Row 3.

Row 31: [K1, yo, k3togtbl, yo, k1] three times, k1, yo, SM, k1.

Rows 33, 35, 37 and 39: As Row 3.

Row 41: [K1, yo, k3togtbl, yo, k1] four times, k1, yo, SM, k1.

Rows 43, 45, 47 and 49: As Row 3.

Row 51: [K1, yo, k3togtbl, yo, k1] five times, k1, yo, SM, k1.

Rows 53, 55: As Row 3.

Row 56: K.

Spiral Shawl charts and instructions continue on page 76.

Spiral Circle made from thick-and-thin chunky yarn.

Wedge Circular Shawl

MATERIALS

12 g / 200 yds cobweb weight yarn

Pair 3.5 mm (US 4) needles

7 Stitch markers

Waste yarn

The original uses ColourMart 100% Cashmere; 1600 yds per 100 g

SIZE

38 cm / 15" diameter

TENSION

26 sts and 50 rows to 10 cm / 4" over centre pattern

CONSTRUCTION

The centre is worked from the centre out, then the lace is added working sideways and removing the stitches of the centre. The live stitches at the start and finish of the lace are then grafted.

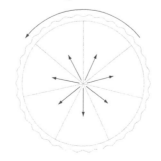

Pattern

THE CENTRE

Cast on 8 sts.

Foundation Row: [K1, PM] seven times, k1.

Work from the Segment Chart, repeating it 7 times per row as follows:

Row 1: [Work from Row 1 of the Segment Chart, SM] seven times, k1.

Work through the 58 rows of the chart in the same way.

Row 59: K2tog, k to end of row. 210 sts

Do not break yarn.

THE LACE

With waste yarn, cast on 10 sts. Change to the working yarn and work from the Lace Chart, noting that each repeat has 12 rows and removes 6 sts from the centre.

Continue until all the centre stitches have been removed. Break yarn, leaving a 12" tail for grafting.

FINISHING

Remove the waste yarn and graft the live stitches of the lace together. Sew Centre seam.

Weave in all ends. Wash and dress.

SEGMENT CHART

Note that ODD ROWS ONLY are charted. On even-numbered rows, knit all stitches

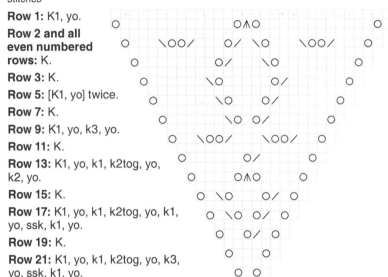

Row 1: K1, yo.

Row 2 and all even numbered rows: K.

Row 3: K.

Row 5: [K1, yo] twice.

Row 7: K.

Row 9: K1, yo, k3, yo.

Row 11: K.

Row 13: K1, yo, k1, k2tog, yo, k2, yo.

Row 15: K.

Row 17: K1, yo, k1, k2tog, yo, k1, yo, ssk, k1, yo.

Row 19: K.

Row 21: K1, yo, k1, k2tog, yo, k3, yo, ssk, k1, yo.

Row 23: K.

Row 25: K1, yo, k4, yo, k3togtbl, yo, k4, yo.

Row 27: K.

Row 29: K1, yo, k5, k2tog, yo, k6, yo.

Row 31: K.

Row 33: K1, yo, k2, k2tog, yo twice, ssk, k3, k2tog, yo twice, ssk, k2, yo.

Row 35: K.

Row 37: K1, yo, k6, k2tog, yo, k1, yo, ssk, k6, yo.

Row 39: K.

Row 41: K1, yo, k6, k2tog, yo, k3, yo, ssk, k6, yo.

Row 43: K.

Row 45: K1, yo, k6, k2tog, yo, k5, yo, ssk, k6, yo.

Row 47: K.

Row 49: K1, yo, k8, yo, ssk, k3, k2tog, yo, k8, yo.

Row 51: K.

Row 53: K1, yo, k3, k2tog, yo twice, ssk, k3, yo, ssk, k1, k2tog, yo, k3, k2tog, yo twice, ssk, k3, yo.

Row 55: K.

Row 57: K1, yo, k12, yo, k3togtbl, yo, k12, yo.

Row 58: K.

LACE CHART

Note that ALL rows are charted.

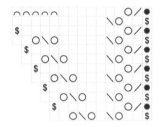

Row 1: S1p, k2, yo, ssk, k1, yo, ssk, yo, k2.

Row 2: S1p, k7, yo, ssk, ktb.

Row 3: S1p, [k2, yo, ssk] twice, yo, k2.

Row 4: S1p, k8, yo, ssk, ktb.

Row 5: S1p, k2, yo, ssk, k3, yo, ssk, yo, k2.

Row 6: S1p, k9, yo, ssk, ktb.

Row 7: S1p, k2, yo, ssk, k4, yo, ssk, yo, k2.

Row 8: S1p, k10, yo, ssk, ktb.

Row 9: S1p, k2, yo, ssk, k5, yo, ssk, yo, k2.

Row 10: S1p, k11, yo, ssk, ktb.

Row 11: S1p, k2, yo, ssk, k10.

Row 12: Cast off 5, k7, yo, ssk, ktb.

Pi Mini Shawl

MATERIALS

55 g / 172 yds DK yarn

Pair 3 mm (US 4) needles

Waste yarn

The original uses ColourMart 50% Cotton, 50% Cashmere; 310 yds per 100 g

Original knitted by Su Lambert

SIZE

45 cm / 18" diameter

TENSION

16 sts and 28 rows to 10 cm / 4" over 144 stitch pattern

CONSTRUCTION

The shawl is worked from the centre out, in the round. Increases are made between the pattern sections, so there are no increases while working the charts.

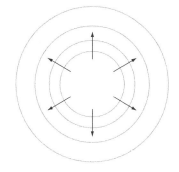

Pattern

Cast on 9 sts into a ring. Join into a circle and knit in the round from now on.

Knit 1 round.

Work the Increase Sequence. 18 sts

Knit 3 rounds.

Work the Increase Sequence. 36 sts

Work the 7 rounds of the 36 st Chart.

Pi Mini Shawl Instructions and charts continue on page 76.

Semi Circular Shawl

MATERIALS

15 g / 260 yds cobweb weight yarn

Pair 3.5 mm (US 5) needles

4 stitch markers

Waste yarn

The original uses North Ronaldsay single ply yarn; 1700 yds per 100 g

SIZE

36 cm / 14" wide by 18 cm / 7" deep

TENSION

20 sts and 40 rows to 10 cm / 4" over pattern

CONSTRUCTION

The shawl is worked from the middle of the long edge out.

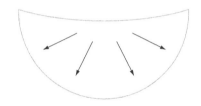

Pattern

With waste yarn, cast on 9 sts.

Foundation Row: K2, [k1, PM] four times, k3.

Now work from the chart, placing 4 repeats in each row as follows:

Row 1: S1p, k1, [work Row 1 of the chart, SM] four times, k3.

Row 2 and all alternate rows: S1p, k to end of row.

Work the 68 rows of the chart.

Cast off LOOSELY.

FINISHING

Remove the waste yarn, placing 4 sts on one needle and 5 on the other. Graft these stitches together to form a continuous garter stitch border.

Weave in all ends. Wash and dress to a semi-circle, pulling out the points formed by the last few rows.

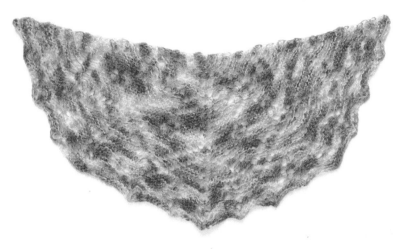

Semi Circular Shawl Chart

Note that ODD ROWS ONLY are charted. On even-numbered rows, knit all stitches.

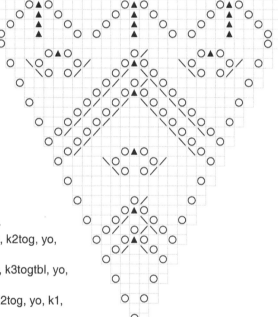

Row 1: K1, yo.

Row 2 and all even numbered rows: K.

Row 3: K.

Row 5: [K1, yo] twice.

Row 7: K.

Row 9: K1, yo, k3, yo.

Row 11: K.

Row 13: K, yo, k3, yo.

Row 15: K.

Row 17: K1, yo, k5, yo.

Row 19: K2, yo, ssk, k, k2tog, yo, k1.

Row 21: K1, yo, k2, yo, k3togtbl, yo, k2, yo.

Row 23: K2, yo, ssk, k2tog, yo, k1, [k2tog, yo, k1].

Row 25: K1, yo, k2, yo, ssk, k1, k2tog, yo, k2, yo.

Row 27: K5, yo, k3togtbl, yo, k4.

Row 29: K1, yo, k4, k2tog, yo, k5, yo.

Row 31: K.

Row 33: K1, yo, k13, yo.

Row 35: K6, k2tog, yo, k1, yo, ssk, k5.

Row 37: K1, yo, k4, k2tog, yo, k3, yo, ssk, k4, yo.

Row 39: K2, yo, ssk, k4, yo, k3togtbl, yo, k4, k2tog, yo, k1.

Row 41: K1, yo, k2, yo, ssk, k9, k2tog, yo, k2, yo.

Row 43: K2, yo, k2tog, k1, yo, k2tog, k7, [ssk, yo, k1] twice.

Row 45: K1, yo, k2, yo, ssk, k1, yo, ssk, k5, k2tog, yo, k1, k2tog, yo, k2, yo.

Row 47: K5, yo, ssk, k1, yo, ssk, k3, k2tog, yo, k1, k2tog, yo, k4.

Semi Circular Shawl chart instructions continue on page 77.

Regional shawls

Shetland "Inside Out"
Shawl
Page 46

Orenburg Shawl
Page 56

Shetland "Outside In"
Shawl
Page 49

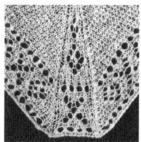

Faroese Shawl
Page 61

Estonian Square Shawl
Page 52

Top-Down Faroese Shawl
Page 62

Estonian Triangle
Page 54

Shetland "Inside Out" Shawl

MATERIALS

16 g / 200 yds cobweb weight yarn

Pair 4 mm (US 6) needles

Thin needle for picking up stitches

Waste yarn

The original uses Alba 1/11.5; 100% Shetland wool; 1280 yds per 100 g

SIZE

46 cm / 18" square

TENSION

20 sts and 40 rows to10 cm / 4" over the centre pattern

CONSTRUCTION

The centre is worked first, then each of the borders separately. The lace is then knitted on sideways.

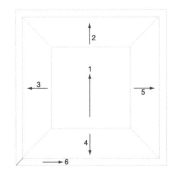

Pattern

THE CENTRE

With waste yarn, cast on 37 sts. Knit 1 row.

Work through the chart.

Do not cast off or break yarn.

FIRST BORDER

Work the border chart directly on from the centre.

Break yarn, leaving a 12" tail. Leave sts on a length of yarn.

SECOND BORDER

Go to the provisional cast on for the

Shetland "Inside Out" Shawl Pattern (continued)

centre. With right side facing, place 37 sts on the needle. Remove waste yarn.

Work the border chart.

Break yarn, leaving a 12" tail. Leave sts on a length of yarn.

THIRD BORDER

Go to one side of the centre. With right side facing, pick up 37 sts on the needle from the s1p loops of the selvage.

Work the border chart.

Break yarn, leaving a 12" tail. Leave sts on a length of yarn.

FOURTH BORDER

Go to the other side of the centre. With right side facing, pick up 37 sts on the needle from the s1p loops of the selvage.

Work the border chart.

Do not break yarn.

LACE EDGING

With waste yarn, cast on 5 sts. Change to the working yarn and work through the Lace Chart, noting that 8 sts are removed from the border for each repeat of the Lace Chart. When all the stitches of that border have been removed, place the stitches from the next border on the needle. Repeat until all the border stitches have been removed.

Break yarn, leaving a 24" tail for grafting.

FINISHING

Remove the waste yarn from the beginning of the lace edging. Graft these sts to the live stitches at the end of the lace. Sew up the mitred corners using whip stitch.

Weave in all ends. Wash and dress.

CENTRE CHART

Note that ALL ROWS are charted.

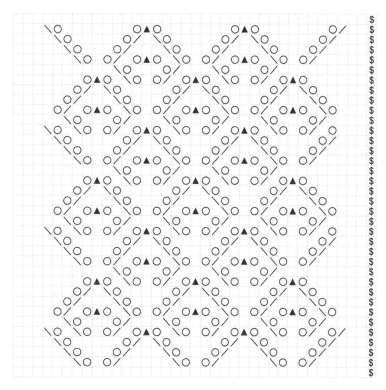

Row 1: S1p, k36.

Row 2: S1p, k to end of row.

Row 3: S1p, k5, [ssk, yo, k1, yo, ssk, k5] three times, k1.

Row 5: S1p, k4, [k2tog, yo, k3, yo, ssk, k3] twice, k2tog, yo, k3, yo, ssk, k5.

Row 7: S1p, k3, [k2tog, yo, k5, yo, ssk, k1] twice, k2tog, yo, k5, yo, ssk, k4.

Row 9: S1p, k2, k2tog, [yo, k1, k2tog, yo, k1, yo, ssk, k1, yo, k3togtbl] twice, yo, k1, k2tog, yo, [k1, yo, ssk] twice, k3.

Row 11: S1p, k4, [k2tog, yo, k3, yo, ssk, k3] twice, ssk, yo, k3, yo, k2tog, k5.

Row 13: S1p, k3, [yo, ssk, k1, yo, k3togtbl, yo, k1, k2tog, yo, k] twice, yo, ssk, k1, yo, k3togtbl, yo, k1, k2tog, yo, k4.

Row 15: S1p, k4, [yo, ssk, k3, k2tog, yo, k3] twice, yo, ssk, k3,

k2tog, yo, k5.

Row 17: S1p, [k5, yo, ssk, k1, k2tog, yo] three times, k6.

Row 19: S1p, k6, [yo, k3togtbl, yo, k1, ssk, yo, k1, yo, k2tog, k1] twice, yo, k3togtbl, yo, k7.

Row 21: S1p, k9, k2tog, yo, k3, yo, ssk, k3, k2tog, yo, k3, yo, ssk, k10.

Row 23: S1p, k5, [k2tog, yo, k1, yo, ssk , k1, yo, k3togtbl, yo, k1] twice, k2tog, yo, k1, yo, ssk, k6.

Rows 25 to 63: Repeat rows 5 to 23 twice more.

Row 65: S1p, k3, [k2tog, yo, k5, yo, ssk, k1] twice, k2tog, yo, k5, yo, ssk, k4.

Row 67: S1p, k2, k2tog, [yo, k7, yo, k3togtbl] twice, yo, k7, yo, ssk, k3.

Row 69: S1p, k to end of row.

Row 70: As Row 2.

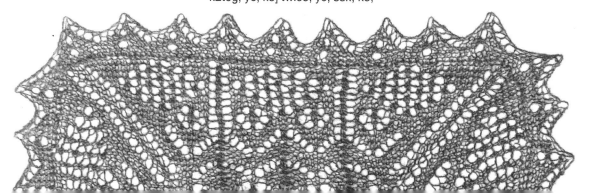

BORDER CHART
Note that ODD ROWS ONLY are charted. On even-numbered rows, knit all stitches.

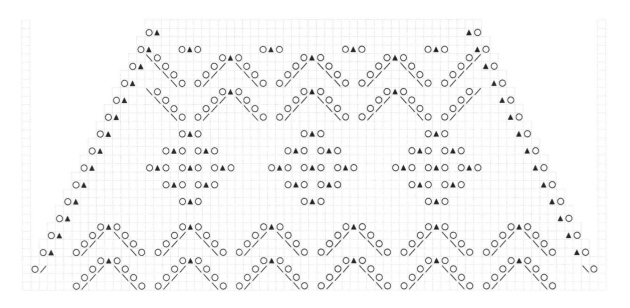

Row 1: K4, [yo, k3, k3togtbl, k3, yo, k1] twice, yo, k3, k3togtbl, k3, yo, k4.

Row 2 and all alternate rows: K.

Row 3: K1, yo, k4, [yo, k2, k3togtbl, k2, yo, k3] twice, yo, k2, k3togtbl, k2, yo, k4, yo, k1.

Row 5: K1, yo, k6, [yo, k1, k3togtbl, k1, yo, k5] twice, yo, k1, k3togtbl, k1, yo, k6, yo, k1.

Row 7: K1, yo, k8, [yo, k3togtbl, yo, k7] twice, yo, k3togtbl, yo, k8, yo, k1.

Row 9: K1, yo, k3, k2tog, [yo, k1, yo, k3, k3togtbl, k3] three times, yo, k1, yo, ssk, k3, yo, k1.

Row 11: K1, yo, k3, k2tog, [yo, k3, yo, k2, k3togtbl, k2] three times, yo, k3, yo, ssk, k3, yo, k1.

Row 13: K1, yo, k3, k2tog, [yo, k5, yo, k1, k3togtbl, k] three times, yo, k5, yo, ssk, k3, yo, k1.

Row 15: K1, yo, k3, k2tog, [yo, k7, yo, k3togtbl] three times, yo, k7, yo, ssk, k3, yo, k1.

Row 17: K1, yo, k7, k2tog, yo, k1, yo, ssk, k1, yo, k3togtbl, yo, k1, k2tog, yo, k1, yo, ssk, k5, k2tog, yo, k1, yo, ssk, k1, yo, k3togtbl, yo, k1, k2tog, yo, k1, yo, ssk, k7, yo, k1.

Row 19: K1, yo, k7, k2tog, yo, k3, yo, ssk, yo, k3togtbl, yo, k2tog, yo, k3, yo, ssk, k3, k2tog, yo, k3, yo, ssk, yo, k3togtbl, yo, k2tog,

yo, k3, yo, ssk, k7, yo, k1.

Row 21: K1, yo, k10, [yo, k3togtbl, yo, k2] twice, yo, k3togtbl, yo, k7, [yo, k3togtbl, yo, k2] twice, yo, k3togtbl, yo, k10, yo, k1.

Row 23: K1, yo, k6, [yo, k3togtbl, yo, k7] four times, yo, k3togtbl, yo, k6, yo, k1.

Row 25: K1, [yo, k5, yo, k3togtbl, yo, k1, yo, k3togtbl, yo, k5, yo, k3togtbl] twice, yo, k5, yo, k3togtbl, yo, k1, yo, k3togtbl, yo, k5, yo, k1.

Row 27: K1, yo, k4, [(yo, k3togtbl, yo, k1) twice, (yo, k3togtbl, yo, k3) twice] twice, [yo, k3togtbl, yo, k1] twice, yo, k3togtbl, yo, k4, yo, k1.

Row 29: K1, yo, k3, [yo, k3togtbl, yo, k1] thirteen times, yo, k3togtbl, yo, k3, yo, k1.

Row 31: K1, yo, k6, [(yo, k3togtbl, yo, k1) twice, (yo, k3togtbl, yo, k3) twice] twice, [yo, k3togtbl, yo, k1] twice, yo, k3togtbl, yo, k6, yo, k1.

Row 33: K1, yo, k9, [yo, k3togtbl, yo, k1, (yo, k3togtbl, yo, k5) twice] twice, yo, k3togtbl, yo, k1, yo, k3togtbl, yo, k9, yo, k1.

Row 35: K1, yo, k12, [yo, k3togtbl, yo, k7] four times, yo, k3togtbl, yo, k12, yo, k1.

Row 37: K1, yo, k23, yo, k3togtbl, yo, k17, yo, k3togtbl, yo, k23, yo, k1.

Row 38: As Row 2.

LACE CHART

Note - ALL rows are charted

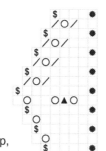

Row 1: K4, yo, k1.

Row 2: S1p, k4, ktb.

Row 3: K5, yo, k1.

Row 4: S1p, k5, ktb.

Row 5: K6, yo, k1.

Row 6: S1p, k6, ktb.

Row 7: K2, yo, k3togtbl, yo, k2, yo, k1.

Row 8: S1p, k7, ktb.

Row 9: K5, k2tog, yo, k2tog.

Row 10: S1p, k6, ktb.

Row 11: K4, k2tog, yo, k2tog.

Row 12: S1p, k5, ktb.

Row 13: K3, k2tog, yo, k2tog.

Row 14: S1p, k4, ktb.

Row 15: K2, k2tog, yo, k2tog.

Row 16: S1p, k3, ktb.

Shetland "Outside In" Shawl

MATERIALS

15 g / 260 yds cobweb weight yarn

Pair 3.5 mm (US 4) needles

Waste yarn

The original uses ColourMart 2/28; Cash/silk/merino; 1400 yds per 100 g

SIZE

38 cm / 15" square

TENSION

26 sts and 50 rows to 10 cm / 4" over centre pattern

CONSTRUCTION

The shawl is knitted from the outside inwards. The lace edging is knitted, then stitches are picked up from the straight edge. The borders are knitted from the lace inwards. The centre is then knitted from the final border, removing the stitches from the side borders as the work progresses. The stitches from the final border are then grafted to the live stitches from the centre. Finally the mitres are sewn and the start and finish of the lace edging grafted.

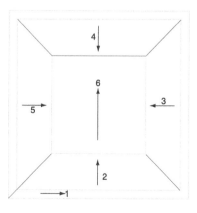

LACE EDGING

With waste yarn, cast on 9 sts. Change to the working yarn. *Work through the 10 rows of the Lace Chart 14 times, then work through the 20 rows of the Lace Corner Chart once. Repeat from * three times more. Break yarn, leaving a long tail. Leave sts on a thread for later grafting.

BORDER

First Border: Pick up and knit 71 sts along one straight edge of the lace. Knit 1 more row. Work through the Border Chart. Break yarn leaving a long tail for grafting. Leave sts on a thread for later grafting.

Second Border: Along the adjacent straight edge, pick up and knit 71 sts. Complete as for the First Border.

Third Border: Along the adjacent straight edge, pick up and knit 71 sts. Complete as for the First Border.

Fourth Border: Along the last straight edge, pick up and knit 71 sts. Complete as for the First Border, but DO NOT BREAK THE YARN.

CENTRE

First, arrange your stitches. Place the stitches from the Third Border on the needle to the right of the live stitches from the Fourth Border. Place the stitches from the First Border on the needle to the left of the live stitches from the Fourth Border.

Now work through the Centre Chart, working the live stitches from the Fourth Border to and fro, and knitting the last stitch of each row together with the first stitch of the remaining stitches of the First and Third Border. When the chart is complete, all the stitches of the First and Third Borders should have been worked off. Break yarn, leaving a long tail for grafting.

FINISHING

Graft the live stitches from the Centre with those from the Second Border. Remove the waste yarn at the start of the lace Edging, and graft those stitches to the final stitches of the Lace edging. Using the long tails of yarn, sew the four mitres of the border, using whip stitch.

Weave in all ends. Wash and dress.

THE LACE CHART

Note that ALL rows are charted.

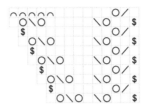

Row 1: S1p, k2, yo, ssk, k1, yo, ssk, yo, k1.
Row 2: S1p, k6, yo, ssk, k1.
Row 3: S1p, k2, yo, ssk, k2, yo, ssk, yo, k1.
Row 4: S1p, k7, yo, ssk, k1.
Row 5: S1p, k2, yo, ssk, k3, yo, ssk, yo, k1.
Row 6: S1p, k8, yo, ssk, k1.
Row 7: S1p, k2, yo, ssk, k4, yo, ssk, yo, k1.
Row 8: S1p, k9, yo, ssk, k1.
Row 9: S1p, k2, yo, ssk, k5, yo, ssk, yo, k1.
Row 10: Cast off 5, k5, yo, ssk, k1.

LACE CORNER CHART

Note that ALL rows are charted.

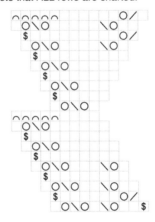

Row 1: S1p, k2, yo, ssk, k1, yo, ssk, yo, k1.
Row 2: S1p, k6, yo, ssk, turn.
Row 3: K2, yo, ssk, k2, yo, ssk, yo, k1.
Row 4: S1p, k8, turn.
Row 5: K1, yo, ssk, k3, yo, ssk, yo, k1.
Row 6: S1p, k8, turn.
Row 7: K6, yo, ssk, yo, k1.
Row 8: S1p, k8, turn.
Row 9: K6, yo, ssk, yo, k1.
Row 10: Cast off 5, k3, turn.
Row 11: K1, yo, ssk, yo, k1.
Row 12: S1p, k5, turn.
Row 13: K3, yo, ssk, yo, k1.
Row 14: S1p, k7, turn.
Row 15: K5, yo, ssk, yo, k1.
Row 16: S1p, k9, turn.
Row 17: K1, yo, ssk, k4, yo, ssk, yo, k1.
Row 18: S1p, k9, yo, ssk, turn.
Row 19: K2, yo, ssk, k5, yo, ssk, yo, k1.
Row 20: Cast off 5, k5, yo, ssk, k1.

BORDER CHART

Note that ALL rows are charted.

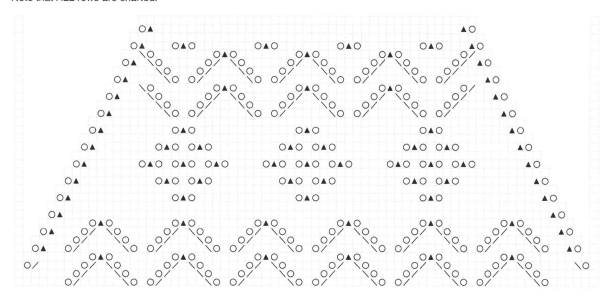

Row 1: K6, *yo, ssk, k5, k2tog, yo, k1. Repeat from * to last 5 sts, k5.

Row 2: K5, *k2, yo, ssk, k3, k2tog, yo, k1. Repeat from * to last 6 sts, k6.

Row 3: K1, yo, ssk, k3, *k2, yo, ssk, k1, k2tog, yo, k3. Repeat from * to last 5 sts, k2, k2tog, yo, k1.

Row 4: K5, *k4, yo, k3togtbl, yo, k3. Repeat from * to last 6 sts, k6.

Row 5: K1, yo, k3togtbl, k2, *yo, ssk, k5, k2tog, yo, k1. Repeat from * to last 5 sts, k1, k3togtbl, yo, k1.

Row 6: K4, *k2, yo, ssk, k3, k2tog, yo, k1. Repeat from * to last 5 sts, k5.

Row 7: K1, yo, k3togtbl, k1, *k2, yo, ssk, k1, k2tog, yo, k3. Repeat from ^ to last 5 sts, k1, k3togtbl, yo, k1.

Row 8: K3, *k4, yo, k3togtbl, yo, k3. Repeat from * to last 4 sts, k4.

Row 9: K1, yo, k3togtbl, k to last 4 sts, k3togtbl, yo, k1.

Row 10: K.

Row 11: K1, yo, k3togtbl, *k12, yo, k3togtbl, yo. Repeat from * twice more, k12, k3togtbl, yo, k1.

Row 12: K.

Row 13: K1, yo, k3togtbl, k9, *[yo, k3togtbl, yo, k1] twice, k7. Repeat from * twice more, k1, k3togtbl, yo, k1.

Shetland "Outside In" Shawl Border Chart Instructions continue on page 77.

CENTRE CHART

Note that ALL rows are charted.

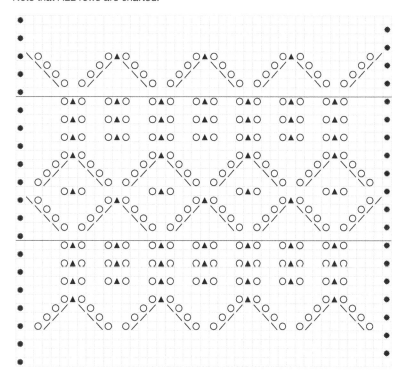

Rows 1 to 4: K42, ktb.

Row 5: K1, *k1, yo, ssk, k5, k2tog, yo. Repeat from * three times more, k1, ktb.

Row 6: K1, *k2, yo, ssk, k3, k2tog, yo, k1. Repeat from * three times more, k1, ktb.

Row 7: K1, *k3, yo, ssk, k1, k2tog, yo, k2. Repeat from * three times more, k1, ktb.

Row 8: K1, *k4, yo, k3togtbl, yo, k3. Repeat from * three times more, k1, ktb.

Row 9: As Row 1.

Row 10: K5, *yo, k3togtbl, yo, k2. Repeat from * six times more, k2, ktb.

Shetland "Outside In" Shawl Centre Chart Instructions continue on page 78.

Estonian Square Shawl

MATERIALS

8 g / 100 yds cobweb weight yarn

Pair 3.25 mm (US 3) needles

Pair 3 mm (US 2) needle

The original uses ColourMart 2/28;
100% Cashmere; 1556 yds per 100 g

SIZE

28 cm / 11" square

TENSION

28 sts and 32 rows to 10 cm / 4"
over centre pattern

CONSTRUCTION

The centre is knitted first, then the
lace is knitted separately in two
pieces and sewn on.

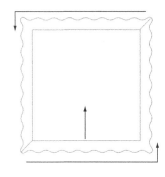

Pattern

CENTRE

With 3.25 mm needles, cast on 61
sts. Change to 3 mm needles and
knit 4 rows. Work the 24 rows of the
chart three times. Knit 3 rows.

Cast off as follows: K2, *return the
2 sts to the full needle and knit
them together through the back
of the loops, k1. Repeat until 1 sts
remains, break yarn leaving a long
tail, and draw through.

Estonian Square Shawl pattern
instructions continue on page 78.

Estonian Square Shawl pattern instructions continue on page 78.

CENTRE CHART

Note that ODD numbered rows only are charted. Even numbered rows are worked: S1p, k2, p to last 3, k3.
A larger version of the chart only appears on page 82.

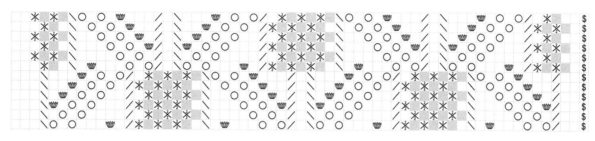

Row 1: S1p, k1, *k1, k2tog, yo, k1, yo, k3, MN, k1, ssk, k1, G2 three times, k2tog, k1, MN, k3, yo, k1, yo, ssk. Repeat from * once, k3.

Row 2 and all alternate rows: S1p, k2, p to last 3 sts, k3.

Row 3: S1p, k1, *k1, k2tog, k1, yo, k1, yo, k4, ssk, G2 three times, k1, k2tog, k4, yo, k1, yo, k1, ssk. Repeat from * once, k3.

Row 5: S1p, k1, *k1, k2tog, MN, k1, yo, k1, yo, k3, ssk, k1, G2 three times, k2tog, k3, yo, k1, yo, k1, MN, ssk. Repeat from * once, k3.

Row 7: S1p, k1, *k1, k2tog, k1, MN, k1, yo, k1, yo, k2, ssk, G2 three times, k1, k2tog, k2, yo, k1, yo, k1, MN, k1, ssk. Repeat from * once, k3.

Row 9: S1p, k1, *k1, k2tog, k2, MN, k1, yo, k1, yo, k1, ssk, k1, G2 three times, k2tog, k1, yo, k1, yo, k1, MN, k2, ssk. Repeat from * once, k3.

Row 11: S1p, k1, *k1, k2tog, k3, MN, k1, yo, k1, yo, ssk, G2 three times, k1, k2tog, yo, k1, yo, k1, MN, k3, ssk. Repeat from * once, k3.

Row 13: S1p, k1, G2 twice, *k2tog, k1, MN, k3, yo, k1, yo, ssk k1, k2tog, yo, k1, yo, k3, MN, k1, ssk*, k1, G2 three times. Repeat from * to * once, k1, G2, k3.

Row 15: S1p, k2, G2, k1, *k2tog, k4, yo, k1, yo, k1, ssk, k1, k2tog, k1, yo, k1, yo, k4, ssk*, G2 three times, k1. Repeat from * to * once, G2 twice, k2.

Row 17: S1p, k1, G2 twice, *k2tog, k3, yo, k1, yo, k1, MN, ssk, k1, k2tog, MN, k1, yo, k1, yo, k3, ssk*, k1, G2 three times. Repeat from * to * once, k1, G2, k3.

Row 19: S1p, k2, G2, k1, *k2tog, k2, yo, k1, yo, k1, MN, k1, ssk, k1, k2tog, k1, MN, k1, yo, k1, yo, k2, ssk*, G2 three times, k1. Repeat from * to * once, G2 twice, k2.

Row 21: S1p, k1, G2 twice, *k2tog, k1, yo, k1, yo, k1, MN, k2, ssk, k1, k2tog, k2, MN, k1, yo, k1, yo, k1, ssk*, k1, G2 three times. Repeat from * to * once, k1, G2, k3.

Row 23: S1p, k2, G2, k1, *k2tog, yo, k1, yo, k1, MN, k3, ssk, k1, k2tog, k3, MN, k1, yo, k1, yo, ssk*, G2 three times, k1. Repeat from * to * once, G2 twice, k2.

Row 24: As Row 2.

LACE CHART

Note that ODD ROWS ONLY are charted.
A larger version of this chart appears on page 81.

Row 1: K.

Row 2 and all alternate rows: K.

Row 3: Ssk, k3, *yo, k1, yo, k3, k3togtbl, k3. Repeat from * to the last 6 sts, yo, k1, yo, k3, k2tog.

Row 5: Ssk, k2, *yo, k1, MN, k1, yo, k2, k3togtbl, k2. Repeat from * to last 7 sts, yo, k1, MN, k1, yo, k2, k2tog.

Row 7: Ssk, k1, *yo, k1, MN, k1, MN, k1, yo, k1, k3togtbl, k1. Repeat from * to last 8 sts, yo, k1, MN, k1, MN, k1, yo, k1, k2tog.

Row 9: Ssk, *yo, k7, yo, k3togtbl. Repeat from * to last 9 sts, yo, k7, yo, k2tog.

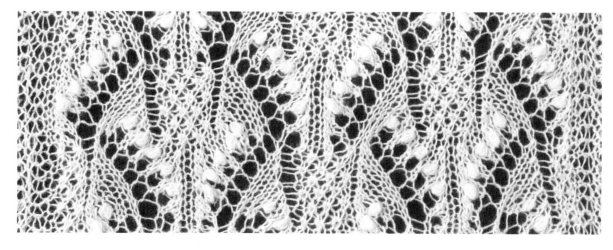

Estonian Triangle

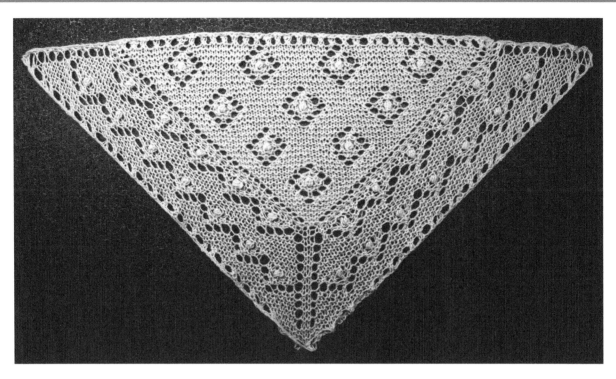

MATERIALS

75 g / 165 yds DK yarn

Pair 6 mm (US 10) needles

3 stitch markers

The original uses Artesano Alpaca DK; 100% Alpaca; 218 yds per 100 g

SIZE

95 cm / 38" by 38 cm / 15"

TENSION

13 sts and 28 rows to 10 cm / 4" over centre pattern

CONSTRUCTION

The centre is knitted first from the tip up. The loops from the row ends are picked up and the borders are knitted on outwards.

Pattern

CENTRE

Cast on 5 sts. Knit 1 row.

Work through the Centre Chart.

Cast off.

BORDER

Pick up and knit 36 loops down one side of the centre, PM, pick up and knit 36 loops up the other side of the centre.

Work from the chart, placing the chart twice per row as follows:

Row 1: S1p, work Row 1 of the Border Chart, SM, work Row 1 of the Border Chart, k1.

Row 2: S1p, k to end of row.

Continue in this way until all 30 rows of the Border Chart have been worked.

Cast off loosely.

FINISHING

Weave in all ends. Wash and dress.

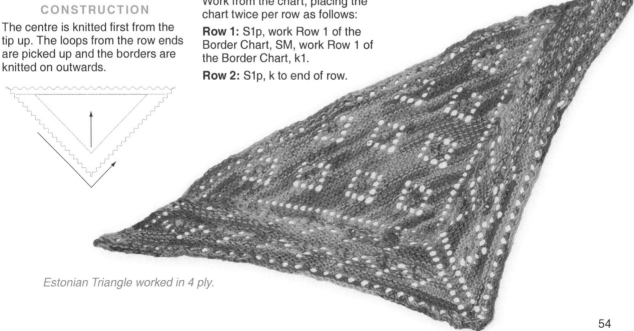

Estonian Triangle worked in 4 ply.

TRIANGLE CHART

Note that ODD ROWS ONLY are charted. Even numbered rows should be worked: S1p, k to end of row.

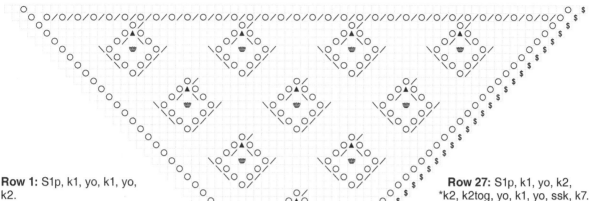

Row 1: S1p, k1, yo, k1, yo, k2.

Rows 2 and all alternate rows: S1p, k to end of row, purling the 7 sts of any nupps together.

Row 3: S1p, k1, yo, k3, yo, k2.

Row 5: Sp1, k1, yo, k5, yo, k2.

Row 7: S1p, k1, yo, k7, yo, k2.

Row 9: S1p, k1, yo, k9, yo, k2.

Row 11: S1p, k1, yo, k4, k2tog, yo, k5, yo, k2.

Row 13: S1p, k1, yo, k4, k2tog, yo, k1, yo, ssk, k4, yo, k2.

Row 15: S1p, k1, yo, k4, k2tog, yo, k3, yo, ssk, k4, yo, k2.

Row 17: S1p, k1, yo, k4, k2tog, yo, k2, MN, k2, yo, ssk, k4, yo, k2.

Row 19: S1p, k1, yo, k7, yo, ssk, k1, k2tog, yo, k7, yo, k2.

Row 21: S1p, k1, yo, k9, yo, k3togtbl, yo, k9, yo, k2.

Row 23: S1p, k1, yo, k10, k2tog, yo, k11, yo, k2.

Row 25: S1p, k1, yo, k1, *k3, k2tog, yo, k9. Repeat from * to last 12 sts, k3, k2tog, yo, k5, yo, k2.

Row 27: S1p, k1, yo, k2, *k2, k2tog, yo, k1, yo, ssk, k7. Repeat from * to last 13 sts, k2, k2tog, yo, k1, ssk, k4, yo, k2.

Row 29: S1p, k1, yo, k3, *k1, k2tog, yo, k3, yo, ssk, k6. Repeat from * to last 14 sts, k1, k2tog, yo, k3, yo, ssk, k4, yo, k2.

Row 31: S1p, k1, yo, k4, *k2tog, yo, k2, MN, k2, yo, ssk, k5. Repeat from * to last 15 sts, k2tog, yo, k2, MN, k2, yo, ssk, k4, yo, k2.

Row 33: S1p, k1, yo, k5, *k2, yo, ssk, k1, k2tog, yo, k7. Repeat from * to last 2 sts, yo, k2.

Row 35: S1p, k1, yo, k6, *k3, yo,

Estonian Triangle chart instructions continue on page 78.

BORDER CHART

Note that ODD numbered rows only are shown. On even-numbered rows, knit all stitches

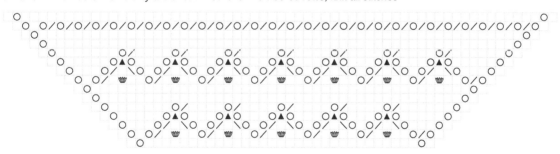

Row 1: K.

Row 2 and all alternate rows: K, purling the 7 sts of any nupps together.

Row 3: K1, yo, [k2tog, yo, k2, MN, k1] five times, k2tog, yo, k1, yo, k1.

Row 5: K1, yo, k2, [k1, yo, ssk, k1,k2tog, yo] five times, k3, yo, k1.

Row 7: K1, yo, k3, [k2, yo, k3togtbl, yo, k1] five times, k4, yo, k1.

Row 9: K1, yo, k4, [k2, k2tog, yo, k2] five times, k5, yo, k1.

Row 11: K1. yo, k to last st, yo, k1.

Row 13: As row 11.

Row 15: K1, yo, [k2tog, yo, k2, MN, k2] seven times, k2tog, k1, yo, k1.

Row 17: K1, yo, k2, [k1, yo, ssk, k1,k2tog, yo] seven times, k3, yo, k1.

Row 19: K1, yo, k3, [k2, yo, k3togtbl, yo, k1] seven times, k4, yo, k1.

Row 21: K1, yo, k4, [k2, k2tog, yo, k2] seven times, k5, yo, k1.

Row 23: As Row 11.

Row 25: As Row 11.

Row 27: K1, yo, [k2tog, yo] twenty-eight times, k1, yo, k1.

Row 29: As Row 11.

Row 30: Cast off LOOSELY.

Orenburg Shawl

MATERIALS

22 g / 300 yds cobweb weight yarn

Pair 3.75 mm (US 5) needles

Thinner needle for picking up stitches

Waste yarn

Row counter

3 stitch markers

The original uses ColourMart 2/28; 100% Cashmere; 1556 yds per 100 g

SIZE

46 cm / 18" square

TENSION

24 sts and 38 rows to 10 cm / 4" over centre pattern

CONSTRUCTION

The bottom edging is worked first, and then stitches are picked up along the straight edge for the centre. The side edgings are knitted along with the centre. The stitches of the centre are worked together with the last stitch of the top edging until only the stitches of the left side edging and the top edging remain. These are then grafted.

Original knitted by Jenny Vowles

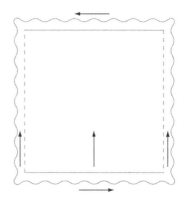

56

Pattern

BOTTOM EDGING

Using waste yarn, cast on 6 sts.

Work through the 16 rows of the Bottom Edging Chart 10 times.

Do not break yarn.

CENTRE AND SIDE EDGINGS

Using a small needle, and starting at the outer (scalloped) edge, remove the waste yarn from the start of the Bottom Edging, putting the stitches on the needle. Place marker. With the same needle, and starting from the cast on end, pick up 80 sts from the straight side of the Bottom Edging. Place marker.

Now working from the first row of the Bottom Centre Chart, work these sts on to the same needle as the stitches left from the Bottom Edging. Thus the 80 sts of the Centre between the two markers are all knit, and the left Side Edging is worked as k3, yo, k3.

You now have both Side Edgings and the Centre on the same needle, and are working all together.

Continue working through the Centre and Side Edgings Charts until all rows of the Bottom, Middle and Top Centre Charts have been completed. Do not break yarn.

TOP EDGING

Work the Top Edging Chart through 10 times, noting that on each odd numbered row you knit the last stitch of the edging with the next stitch of the centre. When the 10th repeat is finished you should be left with the 6 sts of the Left Side Edging only.

FINISHING

Graft the 6 sts of the left Side edging with the 6 st of the Top Edging.

Weave in all ends, using the cast on and cast off tails to neaten the corners. Wash and dress the shawl, pinning out each scallop.

BOTTOM EDGE CHART

Note that ALL ROWS are charted.

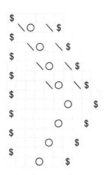

Row 1: S1p, k2, yo, k3.
Row 2 and all alternate rows: S1p, k to end of row.
Row 3: S1p, k2, yo, k4.
Row 5: S1p, k2, yo, k5.
Row 7: S1p, k2, yo, k6.
Row 9: S1p, ssk, k1, yo, ssk, k4.
Row 11: S1p, ssk, k1, yo, ssk, k3.
Row 13: S1p, ssk, k1, yo, ssk, k2.
Row 15: S1p, ssk, k1, yo, ssk, k1.
Row 16: As Row 2.

TOP EDGE CHART

Note that ALL ROWS are charted

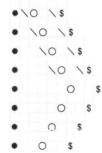

Row 1: S1p, k2, yo, k2, ktb.
Row 2 and all alternate rows: K.
Row 3: S1, k2, yo, k3, ktb.
Row 5: S1p, k2, yo, k4, ktb.
Row 7: S1p, k2, yo, k5, ktb.
Row 9: S1p, ssk, k1, yo, ssk, k3, ktb.
Row 11: S1p, ssk, k1, yo, ssk, k2, ktb.
Row 13: S1p, ssk, k1, yo, ssk, k1, ktb.
Row 15: S1p, ssk, k1, yo, ssk, ktb.
Row 16: K.

SIDE EDGING CHARTS

Note that ALL ROWS are charted. The grey portion represents the Centre charts.

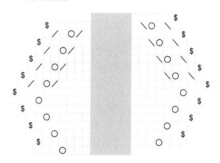

Row 1: K3, yo, k3.
Row 2: S1p, k to Centre, work Centre Chart, k3, yo, k3.
Row 3: S1p, k to Centre, work Centre Chart, k4, yo, k3.
Row 4: S1p, k to Centre, work Centre Chart, k4, yo, k3.
Row 5: S1p, k to Centre, work Centre Chart, k5, yo, k3.
Row 6: S1p, k to Centre, work Centre Chart, k5, yo, k3.
Row 7: S1p, k to Centre, work Centre Chart, k6, yo, k3.
Row 8: S1p, k to Centre, work Centre Chart, k6, yo, k3.
Row 9: S1p, k to Centre, work Centre Chart, k4, k2tog, yo, k1, k2tog, k1.
Row 10: S1p, k to Centre, work Centre Chart, k4, k2tog, yo, k1, k2tog, k1.
Row 11: S1p, k to Centre, work Centre Chart, k3, k2tog, yo, k1, k2tog, k1.
Row 12: S1p, k to Centre, work Centre Chart, k3, k2tog, yo, k1, k2tog, k1.
Row 13: S1p, k to Centre, work Centre Chart, k2, k2tog, yo, k1, k2tog, k1.
Row 14: S1p, k to Centre, work Centre Chart, k2, k2tog, yo, k1, k2tog, k1.
Row 15: S1p, k to Centre, work Centre Chart, k1, k2tog, yo, k1, k2tog, k1.
Row 16: S1p, k to Centre, work Centre Chart, k1, k2tog, yo, k1, k2tog, k1.
Row 17: S1p, k5, k to Centre, work Centre Chart, work Row 1 of this chart.

Repeat from Row 2 to Row 17.

BOTTOM CENTRE CHART

Note that ALL ROWS are charted.

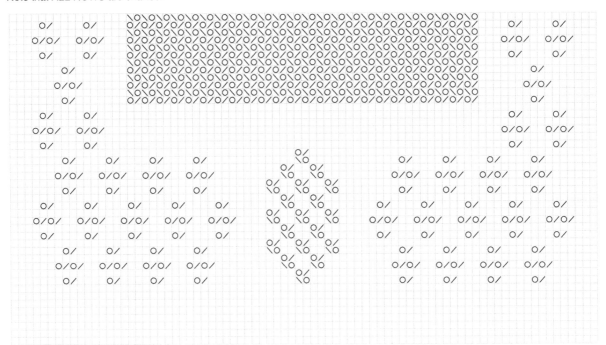

Rows 1 to 8: K.

Row 9: K7, [k2tog, yo, k4] three times, k2tog, yo, k12, yo, ssk, k12, [k2tog, yo, k4] three times, k2tog, yo, k7.

Row 10: K39, yo, ssk, p39.

Row 11: K6, [(k2tog, yo) twice, k2] three times, [k2tog, yo] twice, k9, yo, ssk, k2, yo, ssk, k9, [(k2tog, yo) twice, k2] three times, [k2tog, yo] twice, k6.

Row 12: K37, yo, ssk, k2, yo, ssk, k37.

Row 13: K7, [k2tog, yo, k4] three times, k2tog, yo, k8, [yo, ssk, k2] twice, yo, ssk, k8, [k2tog, yo, k4] three times, k2tog, yo, k7.

Row 14: K35, [yo, ssk, k2] twice, yo, ssk, p35.

Row 15: [K4, k2tog, yo] five times, k7, yo, ssk, k2, yo, ssk, k7, [k2tog, yo, k4] five times.

Row 16: As Row 12.

Row 17: K3, [(k2tog, yo) twice, k2] four times, [k2tog, yo] twice, k4, [yo, ssk, k2] twice, yo, ssk, k4, [(k2tog, yo) twice, k2] four times, [k2tog, yo] twice, k3.

Row 18: As Row 14.

Row 19: As Row 15.

Row 20: As Row 12.

Row 21: As Row 13.

Row 22: As Row 14.

Row 23: As Row 11.

Row 24: As Row 12.

Row 25: As Row 9.

Row 26: As Row 10.

Row 27: [K4, k2tog, yo] twice, k56, [k2tog, yo, k4] twice.

Row 28: K.

Row 29: K3, [k2tog, yo] twice, k2, [k2tog, yo] twice, k54, [k2tog, yo] twice, k2, [k2tog, yo] twice, k3.

Row 30: K.

Row 31: As Row 27.

Row 32: K.

Row 33: K7, k2tog, yo, k7, [k2tog, yo] twenty-four times, k7, k2tog, yo, k7.

Row 34: K16, [k2tog, yo] twenty-four times, k16.

Row 35: K6, [k2tog, yo] twice, k6, [k2tog, yo] twenty-four times, k6, [k2tog, yo] twice, k6.

Row 36: As Row 34.

Row 37: As Row 33.

Row 38: As Row 34.

Row 39: [K4, k2tog, yo] twice, k4, [k2tog, yo] twenty-four times, [k4, k2tog, yo] twice, k4.

Row 40: As Row 34.

Row 41: K3, [k2tog, yo] twice, k2, [k2tog, yo] twice, k3, [k2tog, yo] twenty-four times, k3, [k2tog, yo] twice, k2, [k2tog, yo] twice, k3.

Row 42: As Row 34.

Row 43: As Row 39.

Row 44: As Row 34.

MIDDLE CENTRE CHART

Note that ALL rows are charted.
Chart appears on the next page.

Row 1: [K7, k2tog, yo] twice, [k2tog, yo] twice, k36, [k2tog, yo] three times, k7, k2tog, yo, k7.

Row 2: K16, [k2tog, yo] three times, k36, [k2tog, yo] three times, k16.

Row 3: [K6, [k2tog, yo] twice] twice, k2tog, yo, k36, k2tog, yo, [(k2tog, yo) twice, k6] twice.

Row 4: As Row 2.

Row 5: [K7, k2tog, yo] twice, [k2tog, yo] twice, k8, yo, k2tog, k1, yo, k2tog, [k4, k2tog, yo] twice, k1, k2tog, yo, k8, [k2tog, yo] three times, k7, k2tog, yo, k7.

Row 6: K16, [k2tog, yo] three times, [k17, k2tog, yo] twice, [k2tog, yo] twice, k16.

Row 7: [K4, k2tog, yo] three times, [k2tog, yo] twice, k9, yo, k2tog, k1, yo, k2tog, [k3, k2tog, yo] twice, k1, k2tog, yo, k9, [k2tog, yo] twice, [k2tog, yo, k4] three times.

Row 8: As Row 6.

Row 9: K3, [k2tog, yo] twice, k2, [k2tog, yo] twice, k3, k2tog, yo twice, k2tog, yo, k3, yo, k2tog, k1, yo, k2tog, [k2, k2tog, yo] twice, k1, k2tog, yo, k2, [k2tog, yo]

MIDDLE CENTRE CHART

Note that ALL ROWS are charted. (Written instructions begin on the previous page.)

twice, k4, [k2tog, yo] three times, k3, [k2tog, yo] twice, k2, [k2tog, yo] twice, k3.

Row 10: As Row 6.

Row 11: [K4, k2tog, yo] three times, [k2tog, yo] twice, k2, [k2tog, yo] three times, k3, yo, k2tog, k1, yo, k2tog, k4, k2tog, yo, k1, k2tog, yo, k2, [k2tog, yo] three times, k3, [k2tog, yo] twice, [k2tog, yo, k4] three times.

Row 12: As Row 2.

Row 13: [K7, k2tog, yo] twice, [k2tog, yo] twice, k3, [k2tog, yo] twice, k5, yo, k2tog, k1, yo, k2tog, k2, k2tog, yo, k1, [k2tog, yo, k4, k2tog, yo] twice, k2tog, yo, [k2tog, yo, k7] twice.

Row 14: As Row 2.

Row 15: [K6, [k2tog, yo] twice] twice, k2tog, yo, k13, yo, k2tog, k1, yo, k2tog twice, yo, k1, k2tog, yo, k13, k2tog, yo, [(k2tog, yo) twice, k6] twice.

Row 16: As Row 2.

Row 17: [K7, k2tog, yo] twice, [k2tog, yo] twice, k14, yo, k2tog, k4, k2tog, yo, k14, [k2tog, yo] three times, k7, k2tog, yo, k7.

Row 18: As Row 2.

Row 19: [K4, k2tog, yo] three times, [k2tog, yo] twice, k3, [k2tog, yo] twice, k8, yo, k2tog, k2, k2tog, yo, k7, [(k2tog, yo) twice, k4, k2tog, yo] twice, k4, k2tog, yo, k4.

Row 20: As Row 2.

Row 21: K3, [k2tog, yo] twice, k2, [k2tog, yo] twice, k3, [k2tog, yo] three times, k2, [k2tog, yo] three times, k8, yo, k2tog twice, yo, k7, [k2tog, yo] three times, k3] twice, [k2tog, yo] twice, k2, [k2tog, yo] twice, k3.

Row 22: As Row 2.

Row 23: [K4, k2tog, yo] three times, [k2tog, yo] twice, k3, [k2tog, yo] twice, k21, [(k2tog, yo) twice, k4, k2tog, yo] twice, k4, k2tog, yo, k4.

Row 24: K16, [k2tog, yo] three times, k17, yo, ssk, k17, [k2tog, yo] three times, k16.

Orenburg Square Middle Centre chart instructions continue on page 78.

TOP CENTRE CHART

Note that ALL ROWS are charted.

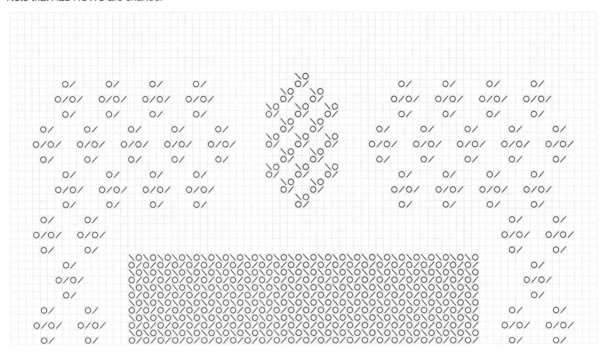

Row 1: [K4, k2tog, yo] twice, k4, [k2tog, yo] twenty-four times, [k4, k2tog, yo] twice, k4.

Row 2: K16, [k2tog, yo] twenty-four times, k16.

Row 3: K3, [k2tog, yo] twice, k2, [k2tog, yo] twice, k3, [k2tog, yo] twenty-four times, k3, [k2tog, yo] twice, k2, [k2tog, yo] twice, k3.

Row 4: As Row 2.

Row 5: As Row 1.

Row 6: As Row 2.

Row 7: K7, k2tog, yo, k7, [k2tog, yo] twenty-four times, k7, k2tog, yo, k7.

Row 8: As Row 2.

Row 9: K6, [k2tog, yo] twice, k6, [k2tog, yo] twenty-four times, k6, [k2tog, yo] twice, k6.

Row 10: As Row 2.

Row 11: As Row 7.

Row 12: As Row 2.

Row 13: [K4, k2tog, yo] twice, k56, [k2tog, yo, k4] twice.

Row 14: K.

Row 15: K3, [k2tog, yo] twice, k2, [k2tog, yo] twice, k54, [k2tog, yo] twice, k2, [k2tog, yo] twice, k3.

Row 16: K.

Row 17: As Row 13.

Row 18: K.

Row 19: K7, [k2tog, yo, k4] three times, [k2tog, yo, k12] twice, [k2tog, yo, k4] three times, k2tog, yo, k7.

Row 20: K39, k2tog, yo, k39.

Row 21: K6, [(k2tog, yo) twice, k2] three times, [k2tog, yo] twice, k9, k2tog, yo, k2, k2tog, yo, k9, [(k2tog, yo) twice, k2] three times, [k2tog, yo] twice, k6.

Row 22: K37, k2tog, yo, k2, k2tog, yo, k37.

Row 23: K7, [k2tog, yo, k4] three times, k2tog, yo, k8, [k2tog, yo, k2] twice, k2tog, yo, k8, [k2tog,

yo, k4] three times, k2tog, yo, k7.

Row 24: K35, [k2tog, yo, k2] twice, k2tog, yo, k35.

Row 25: [K4, k2tog, yo] five times, k7, k2tog, yo, k2, k2tog, yo, k7, [k2tog, yo, k4] five times.

Row 26: As Row 22.

Row 27: K3, [(k2tog, yo) twice, k2] four times, [k2tog, yo] twice, k4, [k2tog, yo, k2] twice, k2tog, yo, k4, [(k2tog, yo) twice, k2] four times, [k2tog, yo] twice, k3.

Row 28: As Row 24.

Row 29: As Row 25.

Row 30: As Row 22.

Row 31: As Row 23.

Row 32: As Row 24.

Row 33: As Row 21.

Row 34: As Row 22.

Row 35: As Row 19.

Row 36: As Row 20.

Row 37 to 44: K.

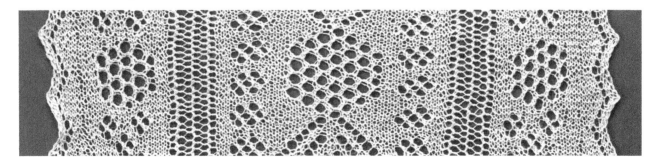

Faroese Shawl

MATERIALS

8 g / 103 yds lace weight yarn

Pair 4 mm (US 6) needles

4 stitch markers

The original uses Alba 1:11.5; 100% Shetland wool; 1280 yds per 100 g

SIZE

46 cm / 18" by 18 cm / 7"

TENSION

26 sts and 48 rows to 10 cm / 4" over garter stitch

CONSTRUCTION

The shawl is knitted from the bottom up. It is made of five sections – a 3 st edging, one main triangle, the back gusset, the second main triangle and the final 3 st border. As the shawl is knitted, the triangles are decreased at the outer edges.

At the same time, starting after the bottom pattern, the gusset is also decreased. Near the top, where the shoulders would come, there are EXTRA decreases in the body of the triangles. These are what keeps the shawl on the shoulders. When all the triangle and gusset stitches have been decreased, the two sets of edging stitches are grafted together.

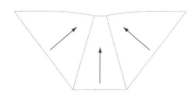

Pattern

Cast on 137 sts.

Row 1: S1p, k to end of row.

Row 2: S1p, k2, PM, k61, PM, k9, PM, k61, PM, k3.

Work the 54 rows of the charts, noting that on each row you work the border, the Wing Chart, the Gusset Chart, the Wing Chart and the border as follows:

Next Row: S1p, k2,SM, work Row 1 of the Wing Chart, SM, work Row 1 of the Gusset Chart, SM, work Row 1 of the Wing Chart, SM, k3.

Pattern instructions are continued on page 79.

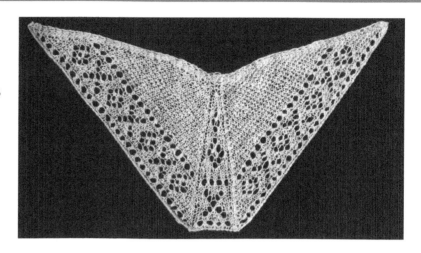

Faroese Shawl Charts

FAROESE WING CHART

Note that ODD ROWS ONLY are charted. On even-numbered rows, knit all stitches. A larger version of this chart appears on page 81.

Row 1: K2tog, k57, ssk.

Row 2 and all alternate rows: K.

Row 3: K2tog, k1, [yo, ssk] twenty-seven times, ssk.

Row 5: K2tog, k53, ssk.

Row 7: K2tog, k6, [k2tog, yo, k3, yo, ssk, k1, k2tog, yo, k2] three times, k2tog, yo, k7, ssk.

Row 9: K2tog, k4, [k2tog, yo, k1, yo, ssk, k2, yo, k3togtbl, yo, k2] three times, k2tog, yo, k1, yo, ssk, k4, ssk.

Row 11: K2tog, [k2, [k2tog, yo] twice, k1, yo, ssk, k1, k2tog, yo] three times, k2, [k2tog, yo] twice, k1, yo, ssk, k2, ssk.

Row 13: K2tog, k3, [yo, k3togtbl, yo, k2, k2tog, yo, k1, yo, ssk, k2] three times, yo, k3togtbl, yo, k3, ssk.

Row 15: K2tog, k2, [k2tog, yo, k2,

k2tog, yo, k3, yo, ssk, k1] three times, k2tog, yo, k3, ssk.

Row 17: K2tog, k41, ssk.

Row 19: K2tog, k1, [yo, ssk] nineteen times, ssk.

Row 21 to 39: K2tog, k to last 2 sts, ssk.

Row 41: K2tog, k4, k2tog, k5, k2tog, k4, ssk.

Row 43: K2tog, k13, ssk.

Row 45: K2tog, k2, k2tog, k3, k2tog, k2, ssk.

Row 47: K2tog, k7, ssk.

Row 49: K2tog twice, k1, k2tog, ssk.

Row 51: K2tog, k1, ssk.

Row 53: K3togtbl.

Row 54: K.

Charts are continued on page 79.

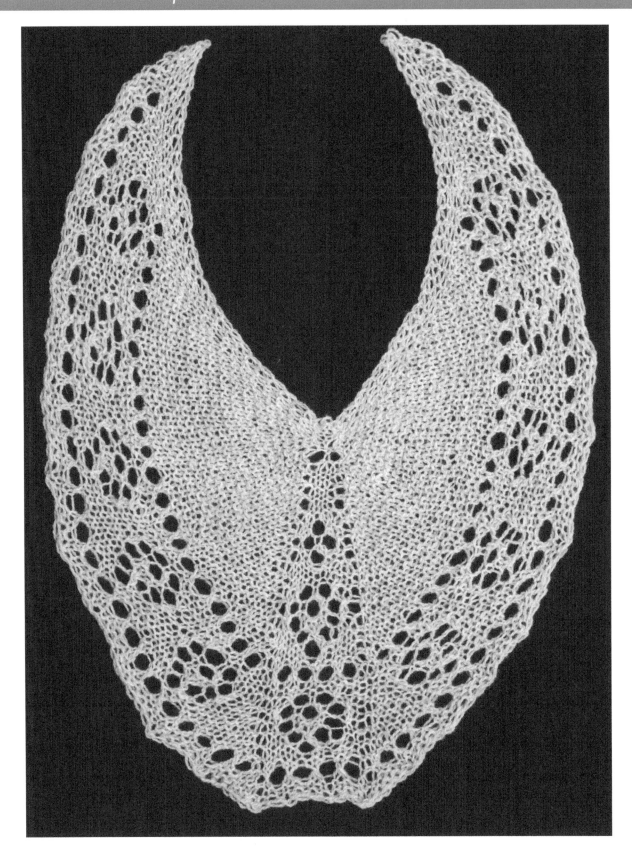

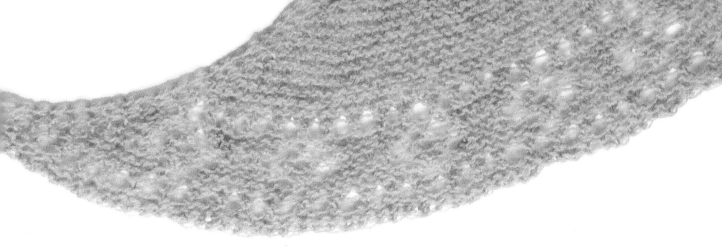

8 g / 103 yds lace weight yarn and pair 4 mm (US 6) needles OR

30 g / 130 yds 4 ply (fingering) weight yarn and pair 6 mm (US 10) needles

4 stitch markers

Waste yarn

The originals use Alba 1:11.5; 100% Shetland wool; 1280 yds per 100 g and Alba 3:11.5; 100% Shetland wool, 427 yds per 100 g

SIZE

Lace Weight - 46 cm / 18" by 18 cm / 7"

4 ply/fingering - 66 cm / 26" by 28 cm / 11"

TENSION

Lace Weight - 26 sts and 48 rows to 10 cm / 4" over garter stitch

4 ply/fingering - 14 sts and 28 rows to 10 cm / 4" over garter stitch

CONSTRUCTION

The shawl is knitted from the top down. It is made of five sections – a 3 st edging, one main triangle, the back gusset, the second main triangle and the final 3 st border.

The shawl starts with a provisional cast on. As the shawl is knitted, the triangles are increased at the outer edges. At the same time, starting after the bottom pattern, the gusset is also increased.

Where the shoulders come, there are extra increases in the body of the triangles. These are what keeps the shawl on the shoulders. When the shawl is finished, the provisional cast on is removed and the two sets of edging stitches are grafted together.

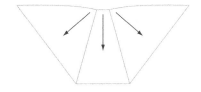

Pattern

With waste yarn, cast on 7 sts. Change to working yarn and knit 1 row.

Set-up Row: K3, PM, m1, PM, k1, PM, m1, PM, k3. 9 sts

Work the 54 rows of the charts, noting that on each row you work the border, the Wing Chart, the Gusset Chart, the Wing Chart and the border as follows:

Row 1: K3, SM, work Row 1 of the Wing Chart, SM, work Row 1 of the Gusset Chart, SM, work Row 1 of the Wing Chart, SM, k3. Cast off LOOSELY.

FINISHING

Remove waste yarn from start. Put 4 sts on one needle and 3 on the other. Graft the two sets of sts together. Weave in ends. Wash and dress, pulling the main parts of the triangles and centre panel into shape (see photo).

Top-Down Faroese Shawl Charts

WING CHART

Note that ODD ROWS ONLY are charted. On even-numbered rows, knit all stitches.

Row 1: Kfb, k1, kfb.

Row 2 and all even nubered rows: K.

Row 3: Kfb twice, k1, kfb twice.

Row 5: Kfb, k to last st, kfb.

Row 7: Kfb, k2, kfb, k3, kfb, k2, kfb.

Row 9: As Row 5.

Row 11: Kfb, k4, kfb, k5, kfb, k4, kfb.

Rows 13 to 34: Repeat Rows 5 and 6 eleven times.

Row 35: Kfb, k, [yo, ssk] to last st, kfb.

Row 37: As Row 5.

Row 39: Kfb, k2, [k2tog, yo, k1, yo, ssk, k4] four times, k2tog, yo, k1, yo, ssk, k2, kfb.

Row 41: Kfb, (k2, [k2tog, yo] twice, k1, yo, ssk) five times, k2, kfb.

Row 43: Kfb, k3, [k2tog, yo, k3, yo, ssk, k2] four times, k2tog, yo, k3, yo, ssk, k3, kfb.

Row 45: Kfb, [k6, yo, k3togtbl, yo] five times, k6, kfb.

Row 47: Kfb, [k7, k2tog, yo] five times, k8, kfb.

Row 49: As Row 5.

Row 51: Kfb, k1, [yo, ssk] to last st, kfb.

Row 53: As Row 5.

Row 55: As Row 5.

Row 56: K.

Charts are continued on page 79.

Extra Patterns

Star Washcloth
(wedge circle)
Page 65

Cat's Paw Washcloth
(diamond square)
Page 67

Bookmark
(stole)
Page 69

Sunhat or Doily
(spiral circle)
Page 70

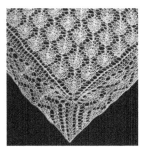

Triangular Scarf
(two tip-up triangles)
Page 72

Star Washcloth

MATERIALS

50g / 108 yds cotton DK

Pair 4 mm (US 6) needles

7 stitch markers

The original uses Tahki Cotton Classic, 100% Cotton; 108 yds per 50 g

SIZE

28 cm / 11" in diameter.

TENSION

24 sts and 32 rows to 10 cm / 4" over garter stitch

CONSTRUCTION

The centre is worked first, to and fro, then the points are worked individually. Finally the centre seam is sewn.

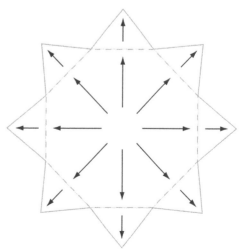

Pattern

THE CENTRE

Cast on 9 sts.

Foundation Row: K1, *PM, k2. Repeat from * three times more.

Work Rows 1 to 25 of the Centre Chart.

Row 26: K2tog, k to end of row.

Now work the points individually:

*****Row 1:** S1p, k1, psso, ssk, k13, k2tog, k1, turn.

Row 2: S1p, k to end of row.

On these stitches only, work through the Point Chart. 3 sts remain.

Next Row: K3tog.

Break yarn and draw through the remaining stitch. Rejoin yarn to the first of the remaining sts.

Repeat from * seven times more.

FINISHING

Sew seam from start of the first point to centre. Close centre hole. Sew in ends, making sure you do this firmly. Wash and dress.

POINT CHART

Note that ALL ROWS are charted.

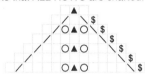

Row 1: S1p, ssk, k4, yo, k3togtbl, yo, k4, k2tog, k1.

Row 2 and all even numbered rows: S1p, k to end of row.

Row 3: S1p, ssk, k9, k2tog, k1.

Row 5: S1p, ssk, k2, yo, k3togtbl, yo, k2, k2tog, k1.

Row 7: S1p, ssk, k5, k2tog, k1.

Row 9: S1p, ssk, yo, k3togtbl, yo, k2tog, k1.

Row 11: S1p, ssk, k1, k2tog, k1.

Row 13: S1p, k3togtbl, k1.

Row 14: S1p, k2.

CENTRE CHART

Note that ODD ROWS ONLY are charted. On even-numbered rows, knit all stitches

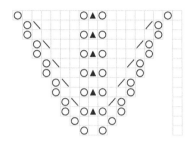

Row 1: K1, *yo, k1.

Row 2 and all even numbered rows: K.

Row 3: *K1, yo, k3, yo.

Row 5: *K1, yo, k1, yo, k3togtbl, yo, k1, yo.

Row 7: *K1, yo, k2tog, k3, ssk, yo.

Row 9: *K1, yo, k2, yo, k3togtbl, yo, k2, yo.

Row 11: *K1, yo, k2tog, k5, ssk, yo.

Row 13: *K1, yo, k3, yo, k3togtbl, yo, k3, yo.

Row 15: *K1, yo, k2tog, k7, ssk, yo.

Row 17: *K1, yo, k4, yo, k3togtbl, yo, k4, yo.

Row 19: *K1, yo, k2tog, k9, ssk, yo.

Row 21: *K1, yo, k5, yo, k3togtbl, yo, k5, yo.

Row 23: *K1, yo, k2tog, k11, ssk, yo.

Row 25: *K1, yo, k6, yo, k3togtbl, yo, k6, yo.

Cat's Paw Washcloth

MATERIALS

20 g / 73 yds 4 ply (fingering) weight cotton or linen yarn

Pair 3.5 mm (US 4) needles

The original uses ColourMart Linen fingering; 361 yds per 100 g

SIZE

About 23 cm / 9" square

TENSION

20 sts and 40 rows to 10 cm / 4" over pattern

CONSTRUCTION

The wash cloth is worked in one piece, from corner to corner.

Pattern

Cast on 3 sts and knit 1 row.

Work through the chart. Cast off.

FINISHING

Weave in all ends.

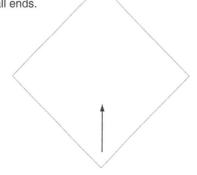

Note that ODD numbered rows only are charted. On even-numbered rows, knit all stitches.

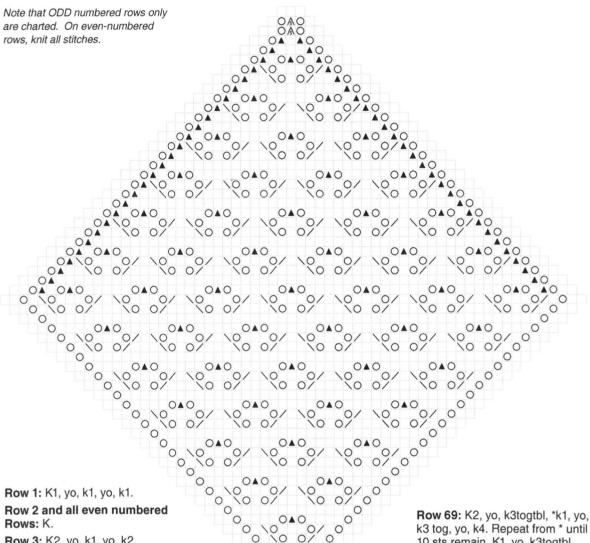

Row 1: K1, yo, k1, yo, k1.

Row 2 and all even numbered Rows: K.

Row 3: K2, yo, k1, yo, k2.

Row 5: K2, yo, k3, yo, k2.

Row 7: K2, yo, k5, yo, k2.

Row 9: K2, yo, k1, k2tog, yo, k1, yo, ssk, k1, yo, k2.

Row 11: K2, yo, k1, k2tog, yo, k3, yo, ssk, k1, yo, k2.

Row 13: K2, yo, k4, yo, k3togtbl, yo, k4, yo, k2.

Row 15: K2, yo, k to last 2 sts, yo, k2.

Row 17: K2, yo, *k1, k2tog, yo, k1, yo, ssk, k2. Repeat from * until 9 sts remain, K1, k2tog, yo, k1, yo, ssk, k1, yo, k2.

Row 19: K2, yo, *k1, k2tog, yo, k3, yo, ssk. Repeat from * until 3 sts remain, K1, yo, k2.

Row 21: K2, yo, *k4, yo, k3togtbl, yo, k1. Repeat from * until 5 sts remain, K3, yo, k2.

Row 23: K2, yo, k to last 2 sts, yo, k2.

Rows 25 to 56: Repeat Rows 17 to 24 four times more (6 'paws' across).

Rows 57 to 60: As Rows 17 to 20.

Row 61: K2, yo, k3togtbl, *k1, yo, k3togtbl, yo, k4. Repeat from * to the last 10 sts, k1, yo, k3togtbl, yo, k1, k3togtbl, yo, k2.

Row 63: K2, yo, k3togtbl, k to last 5 sts, k3togtbl, yo, k2.

Row 65: K2, yo, k3togtbl, *k2, k2tog, yo, k1, yo, ssk, k1. Repeat from * until 6 sts remain, K1, k3togtbl, yo, k2.

Row 67: K2, yo, k3togtbl, *k2tog, yo, k3, yo, ssk, k1. Repeat from * until 12 sts remain, K2tog, yo, k3, yo, ssk, k3togtbl, yo, k2.

Row 69: K2, yo, k3togtbl, *k1, yo, k3 tog, yo, k4. Repeat from * until 10 sts remain, K1, yo, k3togtbl, yo, k1, k3togtbl, yo, k2.

Rows 71 to100: Repeat Rows 63 to 70 five times more. 21 sts remain

Row 101: K2, yo, k3togtbl, k to last 5 sts, k3togtbl, yo, k2.

Row 103: K2, yo, k3togtbl, k2, k2tog, yo, k1, yo, ssk, k2, k3togtbl, yo, k2.

Row 105: K2, yo, k3togtbl, k2tog, yo, k3, yo, ssk, k3togtbl, yo, k2.

Row 107: K2, yo, k3togtbl, k1, yo, k3 tog, yo, k1, k3togtbl, yo, k2.

Row 109: K2, yo, k3togtbl, k3, k3togtbl, yo, k2.

Row 111: K2, yo, k3togtbl, k1, k3togtbl, yo, k2.

Row 113: K2, yo, k5togtbl, yo, k2.

Row 115: K1, yo, k5togtbl, yo, k1.

Row 117: K1, k3togtbl, k1.

Row 118: K.

Bookmark

MATERIALS

2 g / 30 yds cobweb weight yarn

Pair 3 mm (US 3) needles

The original uses 100% Silk hand-spun

SIZE

6 cm / 2.5" by 25 cm / 10" excluding the tassel.

TENSION

15 sts and 20 rows of the pattern measures 6 cm / 2.5" square after washing and dressing.

CONSTRUCTION

The bookmark is worked from the bottom point up.

Chart and instructions appear on page 80.

Pattern

Cast on 3 sts.

Work through the chart, then repeat Rows 15 to 34 three times more.

Knit 5 rows. Cast off.

FINISHING

Weave in cast off tail. Wash and block, running a pair of fine knitting needles through the slipped stitches on each edge of the book mark. (Note – dressing wires are too thick!

Make a tassel with remaining yarn. Attached to the tip of the bookmark when dry.

MAKING TASSELS

Cut a piece of card about 2" deep – or use a credit card! Wind the yarn round it about 20 times, being careful not to wind too tightly. (This stretches the yarn and you end up with a shorter tassel.) Start and stop the yarn at the bottom of the card.

Cut a length of yarn about 24 inches long, and thread it into a wool needle. Tie this tightly round the wound yarn at the top of the card, leaving the free end about the same length as the card. Cut the wound yarn at the bottom of the card. Now use the threaded yarn to wind tightly round the bundle about 1/4 inch down from the knot. Tie this off tightly. Thread the needle back up through to the top of the tassel, and down into the tassel. Trim ends.

Sun Hat or Doily

MATERIALS

50 (65) g / 131 (171) yds DK yarn

Pair 4 mm (US 6) needles

7 stitch markers

18" narrow elastic

2 yards ribbon if required

The original uses Araucania Ruca; 100% Sugar cane; 263 yds per 100 g

This will work for any viscose yarn – e.g. bamboo – or cotton, silk and their blends. You want it cool and floppy!

SIZE

To fit: 0 - 2 years (3 - 8) years

Actual radius: 15 (20) cm / 6 (8)"

TENSION

24 sts and 32 rows to 10 cm / 4" over stocking stitch

CONSTRUCTION

The piece is worked to and fro from the centre out, with the brim being knit on to the crown.

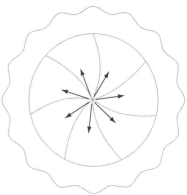

Pattern

BRIM CHART

Note that ALL ROWS are charted.

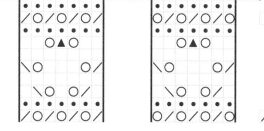

Row 1: K2tog, [yo, k2tog] to end.

Row 2: K.

Row 3: K1, k2tog, yo, k1, yo, ssk, k1.

Row 4: P.

Row 5: K2tog, yo, k3, yo, ssk.

Row 6: P.

Row 7: K2, yo, s1, k2tog, psso, yo, k2.

Row 8: K.

Row 9: K1, [yo, k2tog] to end.

Row 10: K.

Row 11: K2, [yo, k1] three times, yo, k2.

Row 12: Cast off knit-wise.

CROWN CHART

Note that ODD ROWS ONLY are charted. On even-numbered rows, purl all stitches.

Row 1: Yo, k1.

Row 2 and all alternate rows: P.

Row 3: Yo, k to M, SM.

Rows 5 to 24: Repeat Rows 3 and 4 ten times more.

Row 25: Yo, k4, k2tog, yo, k1, yo, ssk, k4.

Row 27: Yo, k4, k2tog, yo, k3, yo, ssk, k3.

Row 29: Yo, k7, yo, k3togtbl, yo, k5.

Chart instructions continue on page 80.

CROWN

Cast on 4 sts.

Row 1: Kfb into each st. 8 sts

Row 2: [K1, PM] seven times, k1.

Now work through the Centre Chart, placing it as follows:

Row 1: (Work the Centre Chart) seven times, k1.

FOR 1ST SIZE:

Work to the end of Row 42 of the chart. 148 sts

FOR 2ND SIZE:

Work to the end of Row 52 of the chart. 190 sts

BRIM (BOTH SIZES)

Work through the Brim Chart.

FINISHING

Sew up back seam. Weave in ends. Sew elastic on the inside above the start of the brim, or thread pretty elastic through the holes in the brim. If desired, thread ribbon through the first holes of the brim and tie in a bow at the side.

Sew elastic on the inside above the start of the brim, or thread pretty elastic through the holes in the brim. If desired, thread ribbon through the first holes of the brim and tie in a bow at the side.

Triangle Shawl

MATERIALS

50 g / 750 yds cobweb weight yarn
Pair 3.25 mm (US 3) needles
3.25 mm (US 3) circular needle for border
2 stitch markers
Waste yarn
The original uses ColourMart 2/30; 100% Merino wool

SIZE

128 cm / 50" wide by 66 cm / 26" deep

TENSION

24 sts and 40 rows to 10 cm / 4" over centre pattern

CONSTRUCTION

The centre is worked first from the tip up. Stitches are then picked up along the two shorter sides and the border is knitted on.

Pattern

CENTRE

Cast on 3 sts.

Work through the chart. Now repeat Rows 29 to 38 until you have 249 sts.

Repeat Rows 13 and 14 twice more. Leave sts on a firm thread.

BORDER

With right side facing, pick up 125 sts from one side of the centre, PM, pick up 1 st from the cast on, PM, pick up 125 sts from the other side of the centre. Knit 2 Rows.

Work through the Border Chart, placing it as follows:

Work through the chart, SM, k1, SM, work through the chart again.

Cast off LOOSELY.

TOP EDGE

With right side facing, pick up and knit 10 sts from the row ends of one border, knit the 249 sts from the top of the centre, pick up and knit 10 sts from the row ends of the other border. Knit 2 Rows. Cast off LOOSELY.

FINISHING

Weave in ends. Wash and dress.

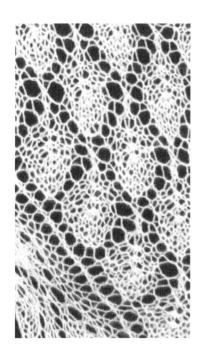

TRIANGLE SHAWL CENTRE CHART

Note that ODD ROWS ONLY are charted. On even-numbered rows, S1p, k to end of row. A larger version of this chart is on page 82.

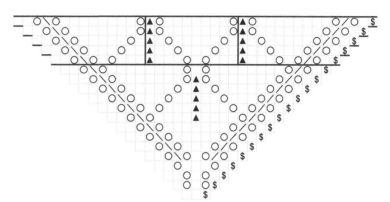

Row 1: S1p, k2.

Row 2 and all alternate Rows: S1p, k to end of row.

Row 3: K1, yo, k1, yo, k1.

Row 5: S1p, k1, yo, k1, yo, k2.

Row 7: S1p, k1, yo, k3, yo, k2.

Row 9: S1p, k1, yo, k2tog, yo, k1, yo, ssk, yo, k2.

Row 11: S1p, k1, yo, k2tog, yo, k to last 4 sts, yo, ssk, yo, k2.

Row 13: As Row 11.

Row 15: As Row 11.

Row 17: As Row 11.

Row 19: S1p, k1, yo, k2tog, yo,

k1, yo, k3, k3togtbl, k3, yo, k1, yo, ssk, yo, k2.

Row 21: S1p, k1, yo, k2tog, yo, k3, yo, k2, k3togtbl, k2, yo, k3, yo, ssk, yo, k2.

Row 23: S1p, k1, yo, k2tog, yo, k5, yo, k1, k3togtbl, k1, yo, k5, yo, ssk, yo, k2.

Row 25: S1p, k1, yo, k2tog, yo, k7, yo, k3togtbl, yo, k7, yo, ssk, yo, k2.

Row 27: S1p, k1, yo, k2tog, yo, k8, yo, k3togtbl, yo, k8, yo, ssk, yo, k2.

Triangle Shawl Centre chart instructions continue on page 80.

BORDER CHART

Note that ODD ROWS ONLY are charted. On even-numbered rows, knit all stitches.

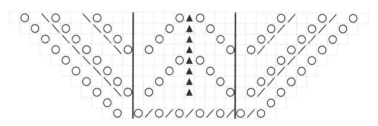

Row 1: K1, yo, *k2tog, yo. Repeat from * to 3 sts before M, k1, yo, k1.

Row 2 and all alternate Rows: K.

Row 3: K1, yo, k to 1 st before M, yo, k1.

Row 5: K1, yo, k1, k2tog, yo, k1, *yo, k3, k3togtbl, k3, yo, k1. Repeat from * to 4 sts before M, yo, ssk, k1, yo, k1.

Row 7: K1, yo, k1, k2tog, yo, k2,

*k1, yo, k2, k3togtbl, k2, yo, k2. Repeat from * to 5 sts before M, k1, yo, ssk, k1, yo, k1.

Row 9: K1, yo, k1, k2tog, yo, k3, *k2, yo, k1, k3togtbl, k1, yo, k3. Repeat from * to 6 sts before M, k2, yo, ssk, k1, yo, k1.

Row 11: K1, yo, k1, k2tog, yo, k4, *k3, yo, k3togtbl, yo, k4. Repeat from * to 7 sts before M, k3, yo,

Triangle Shawl Border chart instructions continue on page 80.

TRIANGULAR SHAWL WITH BORDER & LACE

LACE CHART

Note that ALL rows are charted.

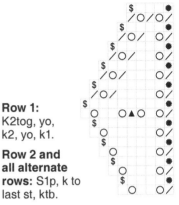

Row 1: K2tog, yo, k2, yo, k1.

Row 2 and all alternate rows: S1p, k to last st, ktb.

Row 3: K2tog, yo, k3, yo, k1.

Row 5: K2tog, yo, k4, yo, k1.

Row 7: K2tog, yo, k5, yo, k1.

Row 9: K2tog, yo, k1, yo, k3togtbl, yo, k2, yo, k1.

Row 11: K2tog, yo, k4, k2tog, yo, k2tog.

Row 13: K2tog, yo, k3, k2tog, yo, k2tog.

Row 15: K2tog, yo, k2, k2tog, yo, k2tog.

Row 17: K2tog, yo, k, k2tog, yo, k2tog.

Row 19: [K2tog, yo] twice, k2tog.

Row 20: As Row 2.

Rows 1 to 20 form the pattern. Repeat them as required.

LACE CORNER CHART

Note that ALL rows are charted.

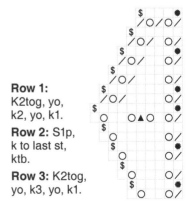

Row 1: K2tog, yo, k2, yo, k1.

Row 2: S1p, k to last st, ktb.

Row 3: K2tog, yo, k3, yo, k1.

Row 4: S1p, k to end of row.

Row 5: K2tog, yo, k4, yo, k1.

Row 6: S1p, k to last st, ktb.

Row 7: K2tog, yo, k5, yo, k1.

Row 8: S1p, k to end of row.

Row 9: K2tog, yo, k1, yo, k3togtbl, yo, k2, yo, k1.

Row 10: S1p, k to last st, ktb.

Row 11: K2tog, yo, k4, k2tog, yo, k2tog.

Row 12: S1p, k to last st, ktb.

Row 13: K2tog, yo, k3, k2tog, yo, k2tog.

Row 14: S1p, k to end of row.

Row 15: K2tog, yo, k2, k2tog, yo, k2tog.

Row 16: S1p, k to last st, ktb.

Row 17: K2tog, yo, k, k2tog, yo, k2tog.

Row 18: S1p, k to end of row.

Row 19: [K2tog, yo] twice, k2tog.

Row 20: S1p, k to last st, ktb.

END-TO-END CRESENT SHAWL

DECREASE CHART

(Chart instructions continued)

Note that ODD rows only are charted. Even-numbered rows are worked as S1p, k to end of row.

Row 8: As Row 2.

Repeat Rows 1 to 8 until 12 sts remain.

Row 1: S1p, k6, k2tog, yo, k2tog, k1.

Row 2 and all alternate rows: S1p, k to end of row.

Row 3: S1p, k1, k3togtbl, yo, k1, k2tog, yo, k2tog, k1.

Row 5: S1p, k3, k2tog, yo, k2tog, k1.

Row 7: S1p, k3togtbl, yo, k1, k2tog, k1.

Row 9: S1p, k2tog, yo, k2tog, k1.

Row 10: As Row 2.

SQUARE SHAWL FROM FOUR TRIANGLES

(Pattern instructions continued)

Row 4: K.

Repeat Rows 1 and 2 once more.

Cast off.

TO WORK IN THE ROUND

Cast on 12 stitches into a ring. Join into a circle.

Foundation Round: [P3, PM] four times

Work from the chart, reading Rounds for Rows, and noting that even numbered rounds are PURL.

FINISHING

Sew seam using whip stitch. Weave in all ends. Wash and dress.

Chart instructions continued

Note that ODD ROWS ONLY are charted. On even-numbered rows, knit all stitches.

Row 29: K1, yo, k4, *k2tog, yo, k3, yo, ssk, k7. Repeat from * to last 12 sts, k2tog, yo, k3, yo, ssk, k4, yo, k1.

Row 31: K1, yo, k5, *yo, ssk, k2tog, yo, k1, k2tog, yo, k7. Repeat from * to last 13 sts, yo, ssk, k2tog, yo, k1, k2tog, yo, k5, yo, k1.

Row 33: K1, yo, k6, *k1, yo, ssk, k1, k2tog, yo, k8. Repeat from * to last 14 sts, k1, yo, ssk, k1, k2tog, yo, k7, yo, k1.

Row 35: K1, yo, k7, *k2, yo, k3togtbl, yo, k9. Repeat from * to last st, yo, k1.

Row 37: K1, yo, k8, *k2, k2tog, yo, k10. Repeat from * to last 2 sts, k1, yo, k1.

Row 38: As Row 2.

Rows 25 to 38 form the pattern. Repeat as required.

SQUARE SHAWL WITH LACE

(Pattern instructions continued)

THE LACE

Slip the 29 live stitches from the centre on to a circular needle, then pick up 31 sts down one side of the centre. Remove the waste yarn and place the 29 sts from the start of the centre on to the circular needle, then pick up 31 sts from the other side of the square.

With waste yarn and a spare needle, cast on 9 sts.

Change to the working yarn, work the Lace Chart, removing the live stitches from the edges of the centre until all have been removed. Break yarn, leaving a long tail for grafting.

FINISHING

Remove the waste yarn from the start of the lace. Graft the start and finish of the lace. Weave in all ends. Wash and dress.

SQUARE SHAWL WITH LACE (CHARTS)

Square Shawl with Lace Charts

CENTRE

Note that ALL rows are charted.

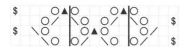

Row 1: S1p, k2, k2tog, yo, *k1, yo, ssk, k1, k2tog, yo. Repeat from * to last 6 sts, k1, yo, ssk, k3.

Row 2: S1p, k1, k2tog, yo, k2, *k1, yo, k3togtbl, yo, k2. Repeat from * to last 5 sts, k1, yo, ssk, k2.

Row 3: S1p, k2, yo, ssk, *k1, k2tog, yo, k1, yo, ssk. Repeat from * to last 6 sts, k1, k2tog, yo, k3.

Row 4: S1p, k3, yo, k3togtbl, *yo, k3, yo, k3togtbl. Repeat from * to last 4 sts, yo, k4.

LACE

Note that ALL rows are charted.

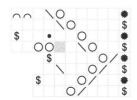

Row 1: S1p, k3, k2tog, yo, k3.

Row 2: S1p, k3, yo, ssk, k2, ktb.

Row 3: S1p, k1, k2tog, yo, k2, ssk, k1.

Row 4: S1p, k4, yo, ssk, ktb.

Row 5: S1p, k2, yo, ssk, k1, yo, yo, k2.

Row 6: S1p, k2, p1, k2, yo, k3, ktb.

Row 7: S1p, k4, yo, ssk, k4.

Row 8: Cast off 2, k1, k2tog, yo, k5, ktb.

DIAMOND SHAWL WITH LACE

(Pattern instructions continued)

the second side, 2 sts from the cast on, 29 sts from the third side and 29 sts from the fourth side. 120 sts

With waste yarn, cast on 6 sts. Change to working yarn and work through the Lace Chart until all the centre stitches have been removed.

FINISHING

Remove the waste yarn and graft the exposed stitches to the live lace stitches. Weave in all ends. Wash and dress.

CENTRE CHART

(Chart instructions continued)

Note that ODD rows only are charted. Even-numbered rows are worked as S1p, k to end of row.

k3togtbl, k2, yo, k8, yo, k2.

Row 47: S1p, k1, yo, k5, k2tog, [yo, k1, yo, k3, k3togtbl, k3] three times, yo, k1, yo, ssk, k5, yo, k2.

Row 49: S1p, k1, yo, k6, [yo, k1, k3togtbl, k1, yo, k5] three times, yo, k1, k3togtbl, k1, yo, k6, yo, k2.

Row 51: S1p, k1, yo, k6, [yo, k2, k3togtbl, k2, yo, k3] three times, yo, k2, k3togtbl, k2, yo, k6, yo, k2.

Row 53: S1p, k1, yo, k3, k2tog, [yo, k1, yo, k3, k3togtbl, k3] four times, yo, k1, yo, ssk, k3, yo, k2.

Row 55: S1p, k1, yo, k4, [yo, k1, k3togtbl, k1, yo, k5] four times, yo, k1, k3togtbl, k1, yo, k4, yo, k2.

Row 57: S1p, k1, yo, k4, [yo, k2, k3togtbl, k2, yo, k3] four times, yo, k2, k3togtbl, k2, yo, k4, yo, k2.

Row 59: S1p, k1, yo, k4, [yo, k3, k3togtbl, k3, yo, k1] four times, yo, k3, k3togtbl, k3, yo, k4, yo, k2.

Row 61: S1p, k1, yo, k3togtbl, k3, yo, ssk, k4, [yo, k, k3togtbl, k, yo, k5] three times, yo, k1, k3togtbl, k1, yo, k4, k2tog, yo, k3, k3togtbl, yo, k2.

Row 63: S1p, k1, yo, k3togtbl, k3, yo, ssk, k2, [yo, k2, k3togtbl, k2, yo, k3] three times, yo, k2, k3togtbl, k2, yo, k2, k2tog, yo, k3, k3togtbl, yo, k2.

Row 65: S1p, k1, yo, k3togtbl, k3, yo, ssk, [yo, k3, k3togtbl, k3, yo, k1] three times, yo, k3, k3togtbl, k3, yo, k2tog, yo, k3, k3togtbl, yo, k2.

Row 67: S1p, k1, yo, k3togtbl, k5, yo, ssk, k4, [yo, k1, k3togtbl, k1, yo, k5] twice, yo, k1, k3togtbl, k1, yo, k4, k2tog, yo, k5, k3togtbl, yo, k2.

Row 69: S1p, k1, yo, k3togtbl, k5, yo, ssk, k2, [yo, k2, k3togtbl, k2, yo, k3] twice, yo, k2, k3togtbl, k2, yo, k2, k2tog, yo, k5, k3togtbl, yo, k2.

Row 71: S1p, yo, k3togtbl, k5, yo, ssk, [yo, k3, k3togtbl, k3, yo, k] twice, yo, k3, k3togtbl, k3, yo, k2tog, yo, k5, k3togtbl, yo, k2.

Row 73: S1p, k1, yo, k3togtbl, k7, yo, ssk, k4, yo, k1, k3togtbl, k1, yo, k5, yo, k1, k3togtbl, k1, yo, k4, k2tog, yo, k7, k3togtbl, yo, k2.

Row 75: S1p, k1, yo, k3togtbl, k7, yo, ssk, k2, yo, k2, k3togtbl, k2, yo, k3, yo, k2, k3togtbl, k2, yo, k2, k2tog, yo, k7, k3togtbl, yo, k2.

Row 77: S1p, k1, yo, k3togtbl, k7, yo, ssk, yo, k3, k3togtbl, k3, yo, k1, yo, k3, k3togtbl, k3, yo, k2tog, yo, k7, k3togtbl, yo, k2.

Row 79: S1p, k1, yo, k3togtbl, [k5, yo, k1, k3togtbl, k1, yo] three times, k5, k3togtbl, yo, k2.

Row 81: S1p, k1, yo, k3togtbl, [k3, yo, k2, k3togtbl, k2, yo] three times, k3, k3togtbl, yo, k2.

Row 83: S1p, k1, yo, k3togtbl, [k1, yo, k3, k3togtbl, k3, yo] three times, k1, k3togtbl, yo, k2.

Row 85: S1p, k1, yo, k3togtbl, k1, yo, ssk, k4, yo, k1, k3togtbl, k1, yo, k5, yo, k1, k3togtbl, k1, yo, k4, k2tog, yo, k1, k3togtbl, yo, k2.

Row 87: S1p, k1, yo, k3togtbl, k1, yo, ssk, k2, yo, k2, k3togtbl, k2, yo, k3, yo, k2, k3togtbl, k2, yo, k2, k2tog, yo, k1, k3togtbl, yo, k2.

Row 89: S1p, k1, yo, k3togtbl, k1, yo, ssk, yo, k3, k3togtbl, k3, yo, k1, yo, k3, k3togtbl, k3, yo, k2tog, yo, k1, k3togtbl, yo, k2.

Row 91: S1p, k1, yo, k3togtbl, k3, yo, ssk, k4, yo, k1, k3togtbl, k1, yo, k4, k2tog, yo, k3, k3togtbl, yo, k2.

DIAMOND SHAWL WITH LACE (CONTINUED)

Row 93: S1p, k1, yo, k3togtbl, k3, yo, ssk, k2, yo, k2, k3togtbl, k2, yo, k2, k2tog, yo, k3, k3togtbl, yo, k2.

Row 95: S1p, k1, yo, k3togtbl, k3, yo, ssk, yo, k3, k3togtbl, k3, yo, k2tog, yo, k3, k3togtbl, yo, k2.

Row 97: S1p, k1, yo, k3togtbl, k5, yo, ssk, k3, k2tog, yo, k5, k3togtbl, yo, k2.

Row 99: S1p, k1, yo, k3togtbl, k5, yo, ssk, k1, k2tog, yo, k5, k3togtbl, yo, k2.

Row 101: S1p, k1, yo, k3togtbl, k5, yo, k3togtbl, yo, k5, k3togtbl, yo, k2.

Row 103: S1p, k1, yo, k3togtbl, k3, yo, k1, k3togtbl, k, yo, k3, k3togtbl, yo, k2.

Row 105: S1p, k1, yo, k3togtbl, k1, yo, k2, k3togtbl, k2, yo, k1, k3togtbl, yo, k2.

Row 107: S1p, k1, yo, [k3togtbl, k1, yo, k1] twice, k3togtbl, yo, k2.

Row 109: S1p, [k1, yo, k3togtbl] twice, yo, k1, k3togtbl, yo, k2.

Row 111: S1p, k1, yo, k3togtbl, k3, k3togtbl, yo, k2.

Row 113: S1p, k1, yo, k3togtbl, k1, k3togtbl, yo, k2.

Row 115: S1p, k1, yo, k5togtbl, yo, k2.

Row 117: S1p, yo, k5togtbl, yo, k1.

Row 119: S1p, k3togtbl, k1

Row 121: S1p, k2tog.

Row 122: S1p, k1.

LACE CHART

Note that ALL ROWS are charted.

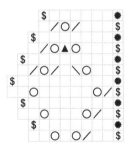

Row 1: S1p, k2, k2tog, yo, k1, yo, k2.

Row 2: S1p, k7, ktog with border.

Row 3: S1p, k1, k2tog, yo, k3, yo, k2.

Row 4: S1p, k8, ktog with border.

Row 5: S1p, k2tog, yo, k5, yo, k2.

Row 6: S1p, k9, ktog with border.

Row 7: S1p, k2, yo, ssk, k1, k2tog, yo, k2tog, k1.

Row 8: S1p, k8, ktog with border.

Row 9: S1p, k3, yo, k3togtbl, yo, k2tog, k1.

Row 10: S1p, k7, ktog with border.

Row 11: S1p, k3, k2tog, yo, k2tog, k1.

Row 12: S1p, k6, ktog with border.

SPIRAL SHAWL

FOR WORKING IN THE ROUND IN STOCKING STITCH

Note that ODD ROWS ONLY are charted. On even-numbered rows, knit all stitches.

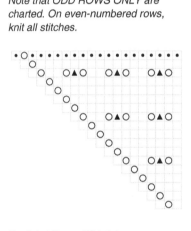

Rnd 1: K1, yo, PM, k1.

Rnd 2 and all alternate Rnds: K.

Rnd 3, 5, 7 and 9: K to M, yo, SM, k1.

Rnd 11: K1, yo, k3togtbl, yo, k2, yo, SM, k1.

Rnds 13, 15, 17, 19: As Round 3.

Rnd 21: [K1, yo, k3togtbl, yo, k1] twice, k1, yo, SM, k1.

Rnds 23, 25, 27, 29: As Round 3.

Rnd 31: [K1, yo, k3togtbl, yo, k1] three times, k1, yo, SM, k1.

Rnd 33: As Round 3.

Rnd 35: P.

Rnd 36: P.

PI MINI SHAWL

(Pattern instructions continued)

Work the Increase Sequence. 72 sts

Work the 16 rounds of the 72 st Chart.

Work the Increase Sequence. 144 sts

Knit 2 rounds.

Work the 10 rounds of the 144 st Chart three times.

Cast off LOOSELY using a needle 2 sizes larger than the working needle.

FINISHING

Weave in all ends. Wash and dress.

PI MINI SHAWL (CHARTS)

Pi Mini Shawl Charts

INCREASE SEQUENCE

Note that all rows are charted

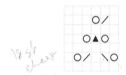

Rnd 1: P.

Rnd 2: *Yo, k1. Repeat from * to end of round.

Round 3: P.

---

36 ST CHART

Note that all rows are charted.

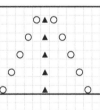

Rnd 1: K.

Rnd 2: *Yo, ssk, k1, k2tog, yo, k1. Repeat from * to end of round.

Rnd 3: K.

Rnd 4: *K1, yo, k3togtbl, yo, k2. Repeat from * to end of round.

PI MINI SHAWL CHARTS (CONTINUED)

Rnd 5: K.

Rnd 6: *K1, k2tog, yo, k3. Repeat from * to end of round.

Rnd 7: K.

---

72 ST CHART

Note that all rows are charted.

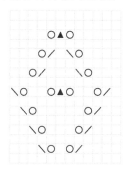

Rnd 1 and all odd-numbered rounds: K.

Rnd 2: *K4, k2tog, yo, k1, yo, ssk, k3. Repeat from * to end of round.

Rnd 4: *K3, k2tog, yo, k3, yo, ssk, k2. Repeat from * to end of round.

Rnd 6: *K2, k2tog, yo, k5, yo, ssk, k1. Repeat from * to end of round.

Rnd 8: *K1, k2tog, yo, k2, yo, k3togtbl, yo, k2, yo, ssk. Repeat from * to end of round.

Rnd 10: *K3, yo, ssk, k3, k2tog, yo, k2. Repeat from * to end of round.

Rnd 12: *K4, yo, ssk, k, k2tog, yo, k3. Repeat from * to end of round.

Rnd 14: *K5, yo, k3togtbl, yo, k4. Repeat from * to end of round.

Rnd 16: K.

---

144 ST CHART

Note that all rows are charted.

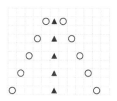

Rnd 1: *K1, yo, k4, k3togtbl, k4, yo. Repeat from * to end of round.

Rnd 2 and all even-numbered rounds: K.

Rnd 3: *K2, yo, k3, k3togtbl, k3, yo, k1. Repeat from * to end of round.

Rnd 5: *K3, yo, k2, k3togtbl, k2, yo, k2. Repeat from * to end of round.

Rnd 7: *K4, yo, k1, k3togtbl, k1, yo, k3. Repeat from * to end of round.

Rnd 9: *K5, yo, k3togtbl, yo, k4. Repeat from * to end of round.

Rnd 10: K.

SEMI CIRCULAR SHAWL

(Chart instructions continued)

Row 49: K1, yo, k5, [yo, ssk, k1] twice, k2tog, yo, k1, k2tog, yo, k5, yo.

Row 51: K8, yo, ssk, k1, yo, k3togtbl, yo, k1, k2tog, yo, k7.

Row 53: K1, yo, k8, yo, ssk, k2tog, yo, k1, k2tog, yo, k8, yo.

Row 55: K3, k2tog, yo, k1, yo, ssk, k3, yo, ssk, k1, k2tog, yo, k3, k2tog, yo, k1, yo, ssk, k2.

Row 57: K1, yo, k1, k2tog, yo, k3, yo, ssk, k3, yo, k3togtbl, yo, k3, k2tog, yo, k3, yo, ssk, k1, yo.

Row 59: K5, yo, k3togtbl, yo, k5, k2tog, yo, k6, yo, k3togtbl, yo, k4.

Row 61: K1, yo, k27, yo.

Row 63: [K1, yo, k3, k3togtbl, k3, yo] three times.

Row 65: K2, [yo, k2, k3togtbl, k2, yo, k3] twice, yo, k2, k3togtbl, k2, yo, k1.

Row 67: K3, [yo, k1, k3togtbl, k1, yo, k5] twice, yo, k1, k3togtbl, k1, yo, k2.

Row 69: K4, [yo, k3togtbl, yo, k7] twice, yo, k3togtbl, yo, k3.

Row 71: P.

Row 72: K.

SHETLAND "OUTSIDE IN" SHAWL

(Border Chart instructions continued)

Row 14: K.

Row 15: K1, yo, k3togtbl, k6, *[yo, k3togtbl, yo, k1] three times, k3. Repeat from * twice more, k2, k3togtbl, yo, k1.

Row 16: K.

Row 17: K1, yo, k3togtbl, k7, *[yo, k3togtbl, yo, k1] twice, k7. Repeat from * once more, [yo, k3togtbl, yo] twice, k7, k3togtbl, yo, k1.

Row 18: K.

Row 19: K1, yo, k3togtbl, k8, [yo, k3togtbl, yo, k12] twice, yo, k3togtbl, yo, k8, k3togtbl, yo, k1.

Row 20: K.

Row 21: K1, yo, k3togtbl, k3, *k3, k2tog, yo, k1, yo, ssk, k2. Repeat from * to last 8 sts, k4, k3togtbl, yo, k1.

Row 22: K6, *k2, k2tog, yo, k3, yo, ssk, k1. Repeat from * to last 6 sts, k6.

Row 23: K1, yo, k3togtbl, k2, *k1, k2tog, yo, k5, yo, ssk. Repeat from * to last 7 sts, k3, k3togtbl, yo, k1.

Row 24: K5, k2tog, yo, k7, *yo, k3togtbl, yo, k7. Repeat from * to last 7 sts, yo, ssk, k5.

Row 25: K1, yo, k3togtbl, k1, *k3, k2tog, yo, k1, yo, ssk, k2. Repeat from * to last 6 sts, k2, k3togtbl, yo, k1.

Row 26: K4, *k2, k2tog, yo, k3, yo, ssk, k1. Repeat from * to last 4 sts, k4.

Row 27: K1, yo, k3togtbl, *k1, k2tog, yo, k5, yo, ssk. Repeat from * to last 5 sts, k1, k3togtbl, yo, k1.

Row 28: K3, k2tog, yo, k7, *yo, k3togtbl, yo, k7. Repeat from * to last 5 sts, yo, ssk, k3.

Row 29: K1, yo, k3togtbl, *k3, yo, k3togtbl, yo, k4. Repeat from * twice, k3, yo, k3togtbl, yo, k3, k3togtbl, yo, k1.

Row 30: K.

Row 31: K1, yo, k3togtbl, k to last 4 sts, k3togtbl, yo, k1.

Row 32: K.

SHETLAND "OUTSIDE IN" SHAWL

(Center Chart instructions continued)

Rows 11 to 14: Repeat Rows 9 and 10 twice.

Row 15: As Row 1.

Row 16: K1, *k3, k2tog, yo, k1, yo, ssk, k2. Repeat from * three times more, k1, ktb.

Row 17: K1, *k2, k2tog, yo, k3, yo, ssk, k1. Repeat from * three times more, k1, ktb.

Row 18: K1, *k1, k2tog, yo, k5, yo, ssk. Repeat from * three times more, k1, ktb.

Row 19: K1, k2tog, yo, *k7, yo, k3togtbl, yo. Repeat from * twice more, k7, yo, ssk, ktb.

Row 20: K1, *k4, yo, k3togtbl, yo, k3. Repeat from * three times more, k1, ktb.

Rows 21 to 83: Repeat Rows 5 to 20 three times more, then 5 to 19 again.

Rows 84 to 87: As Row 1.

ESTONIAN SQUARE SHAWL

(Pattern instructions continued)

LACE EDGING

With 3.25 mm needles and TWO strands of yarn, cast on 101 sts. Break one strand and continue with only one. Work the 9 rows of the chart. Cast off as for the centre.

Make another piece the same.

FINISHING

Pin one piece of the lace long two sides of the centre. Whip stitch in place. Repeat with the other piece. Whip stitch the ends of the lace together.

Weave in all ends. Wash and dress.

ESTONIAN TRIANGLE

(Triangle chart instructions continued)

k3togtbl, yo, k8. Repeat from * to last 3 sts, k1, yo, k2.

Row 37: S1p, k1, yo, k7, *k3, k2tog, yo, k9. Repeat from * to last 4 sts, k2, yo, k2.

Rows 39 to 66: Repeat rows 25 to 38 twice more.

Row 67: S1p, k1, yo, *k2tog, yo. Repeat from * to last 3 sts, k1, yo, k2.

Row 68: S1p, k to end of row.

Row 69: S1p, k to end of row.

Row 70: Cast off LOOSELY.

ORENBURG SHAWL

Middle Centre chart instructions continued

Row 25: K16, [k2tog, yo] three times, k17, yo, ssk, k17, [k2tog, yo] three times, k16.

Row 26: K16, [k2tog, yo] three times, k15, yo, ssk, p2, yo, ssk, k15, [k2tog, yo] three times, k16.

Row 27: K16, [k2tog, yo] three times, k15, yo, ssk, k2, yo, ssk, k15, [k2tog, yo] three times, k16.

Row 28: K7, yo, ssk, k7, [k2tog, yo] three times, k13, [yo, ssk, p2] twice, yo, ssk, k13, [k2tog, yo] three times, k7, yo, ssk, k7.

Row 29: K7, yo, ssk, k7, [k2tog, yo] three times, k3, [k2tog, yo] twice, k6, [yo, ssk, k2] twice, yo, ssk, k5, [k2tog, yo] twice, k4, [k2tog, yo] three times, k7, yo, ssk, k7.

Row 30: K5, yo, ssk, k2, yo, ssk, k5, [k2tog, yo] three times, k11, [yo, ssk, k2] three times, yo, ssk, k11, [k2tog, yo] three times, k5, yo, ssk, kp2, yo, ssk, k5.

Row 31: K5, yo, ssk, k2, yo, ssk, k5, [(k2tog, yo) three times, k2] twice, yo twice, [ssk, k2, yo] three times, ssk, k2, [k2tog, yo] three times, k3, [k2tog, yo] three times, k5, yo, ssk, k2, yo, ssk, k5.

Row 32: K3, [yo, ssk, k2] twice, yo, ssk, k3, [k2tog, yo] three times, k13, [yo, ssk, k2] twice, yo, ssk, k13, [k2tog, yo] three times, k3, [yo, ssk, k2] twice, yo, ssk, k3.

Row 33: K3, [yo, ssk, k2] twice, yo, ssk, k3, [k2tog, yo] three times, k3, [k2tog, yo] twice, k6, [yo, ssk, k2] twice, yo, ssk, k5, [k2tog, yo] twice, k4, [k2tog, yo] three times, k3, [yo, ssk, k2] twice, yo, ssk, k3.

Row 34: K5, yo, ssk, k2, yo, ssk, k5, [k2tog, yo] three times, k11, [yo, ssk, k2] three times, yo, ssk, k11, [yo, ssk] twice, yo, ssk, k5, yo, ssk, k2, yo, ssk, k5.

Row 35: K5, yo, ssk, k2, yo, ssk, k5, [yo, ssk] twice, yo, ssk, k11, [yo, ssk, k2] three times, yo, ssk, k11, [k2tog, yo] three times, k5, yo, ssk, k2, yo, ssk, k5.

Row 36: K3, [yo, ssk, k2] twice, yo, ssk, k3, [k2tog, yo] three times, k13, [yo, ssk, k2] twice, yo, ssk, k13, [yo, ssk] twice, yo, ssk, k3, [yo, ssk, k2] twice, yo, ssk, k3.

Row 37: K3, [yo, ssk, k2] twice, yo, ssk, k3, [yo, ssk] twice, yo, ssk, k13, [yo, ssk, k2] twice, yo, ssk, k13, [k2tog, yo] three times, k3, [yo, ssk, k2] twice, yo, ssk, k3.

Row 38: As Row 34.

Row 39: K5, yo, ssk, k2, yo, ssk, k5, [yo, ssk] twice, yo, ssk, k3, [k2tog, yo] twice, k4, [yo, ssk, k2] three times, yo, ssk, k3, [k2tog, yo] twice, k4, [k2tog, yo] three times, k5, yo, ssk, k2, yo, ssk, k5.

Row 40: As Row 36.

Row 41: K3, [yo, ssk, k2] twice, yo, ssk, k3, [yo, ssk] twice, yo, ssk, k2, [k2tog, yo] three times, k5, [yo, ssk, k2] twice, yo, ssk, k4, [(k2tog, yo) three times, k3] twice, [yo, ssk, k2] twice, yo, ssk, k3.

Row 42: As Row 34.

Row 43: As Row 39.

Row 44: K7, yo, ssk, k7, [k2tog, yo] three times, k13, [yo, ssk, k2] twice, yo, ssk, k13, [yo, ssk] twice, [yo, ssk, k7] twice.

Row 45: [K7, yo, ssk] twice, [yo, ssk] twice, k13, [yo, ssk, k2] twice, yo, ssk, k13, [k2tog, yo] three times, k7, yo, ssk, k7.

Row 46: K16, [k2tog, yo] three times, k15, yo, ssk, k2, yo, ssk, k15, [yo, ssk] three times, k16.

Row 47: K16, [yo, ssk] twice, yo, ssk, k15, yo, ssk, k2, yo, ssk, k15, [k2tog, yo] three times, k16.

Row 48: K16, [k2tog, yo] three times, [k17, yo, ssk] twice, [yo, ssk] twice, k16.

Row 49: [K4, k2tog, yo] twice, k4, [yo, ssk] three times, k3, [k2tog, yo] twice, k10, yo, ssk, k9, [(k2tog, yo) twice, k4, k2tog, yo] twice, k4, k2tog, yo, k4.

Row 50: K16, [k2tog, yo] three times, k36, [yo, ssk] three times, k16.

Row 51: K3, [k2tog, yo] twice, k2, [k2tog, yo] twice, k3, [yo, ssk] three times, k2, [k2tog, yo] three times, k7, k2tog, yo, k2, yo, k2tog, k6, [(k2tog, yo) three times, k3] twice, [k2tog, yo] twice, k2,

Orenburg Shawl Middle Centre chart instructions continued

[k2tog, yo] twice, k3.

Row 52: As Row 50.

Row 53: [K4, k2tog, yo] twice, k4, [yo, ssk] three times, k3, [k2tog, yo] twice, k7, k2tog, yo, k4, yo, k2tog, k6, [(k2tog, yo) twice, k4, k2tog, yo] twice, k4, k2tog, yo, k4.

Row 54: As Row 50.

Row 55: K7, k2tog, yo, k7, [yo, ssk] three times, k13, k2tog, yo, k6, yo, k2tog, k13, [k2tog, yo] twice, [k2tog, yo, k7] twice.

Row 56: As Row 50.

Row 57: K6, [k2tog, yo] twice, k6, [yo, ssk] three times, k12, k2tog, yo, k1, k2tog, yo, k2, yo, k2tog, k1, yo, k2tog, k12, k2tog, yo, [(k2tog, yo) twice, k6] twice.

Row 58: As Row 50.

Row 59: K7, k2tog, yo, k7, [yo, ssk] three times, k3, [k2tog, yo] twice, k4, k2tog, yo, k1, k2tog, yo, k4, yo, k2tog, k1, yo, k2tog, k3, [k2tog, yo] twice, k4, [k2tog, yo] three times, k7, k2tog, yo, k7.

Row 60: As Row 50.

Row 61: [K4, k2tog, yo] twice, k4, [yo, ssk] three times, k2, [k2tog, yo] three times, k2, k2tog, yo, k1, k2tog, yo, k6, [yo, k2tog, k1] twice, [k2tog, yo] three times, k3, [k2tog, yo] twice, [k2tog, yo, k4] three times.

Row 62: K16, [k2tog, yo] three times, k17, k2tog, yo, k17, [yo, ssk] three times, k16.

Row 63: K3, [k2tog, yo] twice, k2, [(k2tog, yo) twice, k3, k2tog, yo] twice, k2tog, yo, k2, k2tog, yo, k1, [k2tog, yo, k3] twice, [yo, k2tog, k1] twice, [k2tog, yo] twice, k4, [k2tog, yo] three times, k3, [k2tog, yo] twice, k2, [k2tog, yo] twice, k3.

Row 64: As Row 6.

Row 65: [K4, k2tog, yo] three times, [k2tog, yo] twice, k8, k2tog, yo, k1, [k2tog, yo, k4] twice, yo, k2tog, k1, yo, k2tog, k8, [k2tog, yo] twice, [k2tog, yo, k4] three times.

Row 66: As Row 6.

Row 67: [K7, k2tog, yo] twice, [k2tog, yo] twice, k7, k2tog, yo, k, [k2tog, yo, k5] twice, yo, k2tog,

k, yo, k2tog, k7, [k2tog, yo] twice, [k2tog, yo, k7] twice.

Row 68: As Row 2.

Row 69: As Row 3.

Row 70: As Row 2.

Row 71: As Row 1.

Row 72: As Row 2.

FAROESE SHAWL

Pattern instructions continued

Remove markers on the last row. 9 sts remain.

Row 55: S1p, k2, k3togtbl, k3.

Break yarn leaving a long tail for grafting.

FINISHING

Put 4 sts on one needle and 3 on the other. Graft the two sets of sts together. Weave in ends. Wash and dress, pulling the main parts of the triangles and centre panel into shape (see photo).

GUSSET CHART

Note that ODD ROWS ONLY are shown. On even-numbered rows, knit all stitches.

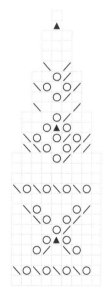

Row 1: K.

Row 2 and all alternate rows: K.

Row 3: K1, [yo, ssk] four times.

Row 5: K.

Row 7: K2, yo, ssk, k1, k2tog, yo, k2.

Row 9: K3, yo, k3togtbl, yo, k3.

Row 11: K3, k2tog, yo, k4.

Row 13: K2, k2tog, yo, k1, yo, ssk, k2.

Row 15: K1, k2tog, yo, k3, yo, ssk, k1.

Row 17: K.

Row 19: As Row 3.

Rows 21 and 23: K.

Row 25: K3, k2tog, yo, k4.

Row 27: K2tog twice, yo, k1, yo, ssk twice.

Row 29: [k2tog, yo] twice, k1, yo, ssk.

Row 31: K2, yo, k3togtbl, yo, k2.

Row 33: K2, k2tog, yo, k3.

Row 35: K2tog, k3, ssk.

Row 37: K1, k2tog, yo, k2.

Row 39: K2tog, yo, k1, yo, ssk.

Row 41: Repeat Row 37.

Row 43: K2tog, k1, ssk.

Rows 45 to 49: K.

Row 51: K3togtbl.

Row 53: K.

Row 54: K.

TOP-DOWN FAROESE SHAWL

GUSSET CHART

Note that ODD ROWS ONLY are shown. On even-numbered rows, knit all stitches.

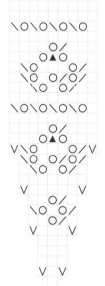

Row 1: K.

Row 2 and all alternate rows: K.

Row 3: Kfb, k1, kfb.

Rows 5, 7 and 9: K.

Row 11: Kfb, k3, kfb.

Row 13: K1, k2tog, yo, k2.

Row 15: K2tog, yo, k1, yo, ssk.

Row 17: As Row 13.

Row 19: Kfb, k5, kfb.

Row 21: K.

Row 23: K1, k2tog, yo, k1, yo, ssk, k1.

Row 25: [K2tog, yo] twice, k1, yo, ssk.

Row 27: Kfb, k2tog, yo, k3, yo, ssk, kfb.

Row 29: K3, yo, k3togtbl, yo, k3.

Row 31: K3, k2tog, yo, k4.

Row 33: K.

Row 35: K1, [yo, ssk] four times.

Row 37: K.

Row 39: K2, k2tog, yo, k1, yo, ssk, k2.

Row 41: K1, [k2tog, yo] twice, k1, yo, ssk, k1.

Row 43: K1, k2tog, yo, k3, yo, ssk, k.1

Row 45: As Row 29.

Row 47: As Row 31.

Row 49: K.

Row 51: As Row 35.

Rows 52 to 56: K.

BOOKMARK

Bookmark Chart

Note that ODD ROWS ONLY are charted.

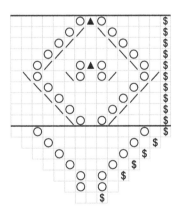

Row 1: S1p, k2.

Row 2 and all following even numbered rows: S1p, k to end of row.

Row 3: K1, yo, k1, yo, k1. 5 sts

Row 5: S1p, (k1, yo) twice, k2. 7 sts

Row 7: S1p, k1, yo, k3, yo, k2. 9 sts

Row 9: S1p, k1, yo, k5, yo, k2. 11 sts

Row 11: S1p, k1, yo, k7, yo, k2. 13 sts

Row 13: S1p, k1, yo, k9, yo, k2. 15 sts.

Row 15: S1p, k4, k2tog, yo, k1, yo, ssk, k5.

Row 17: S1p, k3, k2tog, yo, k3, yo, ssk, k4.

Row 19: S1p, k2, k2tog, yo, k5, yo, ssk, k3.

Row 21: S1p, k1, k2tog, yo, k7, yo, ssk, k2.

Row 23: S1p, k2tog, yo, k2, k2tog, yo, k1, yo, ssk, k2, yo, ssk, k1.

Row 25: S1p, k1, yo, ssk, k2, yo, k3togtbl, yo, k2, k2tog, yo, k2.

Row 27: S1p, k2, yo, ssk, k5, k2tog, yo, k3.

Row 29: S1p, k3, yo, ssk, k3, k2tog, yo, k4.

Row 31: S1p, k4, yo, ssk, k1, k2tog, yo, k5.

Row 33: S1p, k5, yo, k3togtbl, yo, k6.

Row 34: S1p, k14.

Rows 15 to 34 form the pattern. Repeat them as necessary.

SUNHAT OR DOILY

Centre chart instructions continued

Rows 31 to 42: Repeat Rows 3 and 4 six times.

2ND SIZE ONLY:

Row 43: Yo, k4, k2tog, yo, k1, yo, ssk, k4, k2tog, yo, k1, yo, k4.

Row 45: Yo, k4, k2tog, yo, k3, yo, ssk, k2, k2tog, yo, k3, yo, ssk, k3.

Row 47: Yo, k7, yo, s1, k2tog, psso, yo, k6, yo, s1, k2tog, psso, yo, k5.

Row 49 to 52: Repeat Rows 3 and 4 twice more.

TRIANGLE SHAWL

Centre chart instructions continued

Row 29: S1p, k1, yo, k2tog, yo, k1, *yo, k3, k3togtbl, k3, yo, k1. Repeat from * until 4 sts remain, yo, ssk, yo, k2.

Row 31: S1p, k1, yo, k2tog, yo, k2, *k1, yo, k2, k3togtbl, k2, yo, k2. Repeat from * until 5 sts remain, k1, yo, ssk, yo, k2.

Row 33: S1p, k1, yo, k2tog, yo, k3, *k2, yo, k1, k3togtbl, k1, yo, k3. Repeat from * until 6 sts remain, k2, yo, ssk, yo, k2.

Row 35: S1p, k1, yo, k2tog, yo, k4, *k3, yo, k3togtbl, yo, k4. Repeat from * until 7 sts remain, k3, yo, ssk, yo, k2.

Row 37: S1p, k1, yo, k2tog, yo, k5, *k3, yo, k3togtbl, yo, k4. Repeat from * until 8 sts remain, k4, yo, ssk, yo, k2.

Row 38: S1p, k to end of row.

Border chart instructions continued

ssk, k1, yo, k1.

Row 13: K1, yo, k1, k2tog, yo, k2, k2tog, yo, k1, *yo, k3, k3togtbl, k3, yo, k1. Repeat from * to 8 sts before M, yo, ssk, k2, yo, ssk, 13k1, yo, k1.

Row 15: K1, yo, k1, k2tog, yo, k2, k2tog, yo, k2, *k1, yo, k2, k3togtbl, k2, yo, k2. Repeat from * to 9 sts before M, k1, yo, ssk, k2, yo, ssk, k1, yo, k1.

Row 17: K1, yo, k1, k2tog, yo, k2, k2tog, yo, k3, *k2, yo, k1, k3togtbl, k1, yo, k3. Repeat from * to 10 sts before M, k2, yo, ssk, k2, yo, ssk, k1, yo, k1.

Row 19: K1, yo, k1, k2tog, yo, k2, k2tog, yo, k4, *k3, yo, k3togtbl, yo, k4. Repeat from * to 11 sts before M, k3, yo, ssk, k2, yo, ssk, k1, yo, k1.

Row 20: K.

Charts Shown Larger

MINI FISCHOU CHART (LARGER)

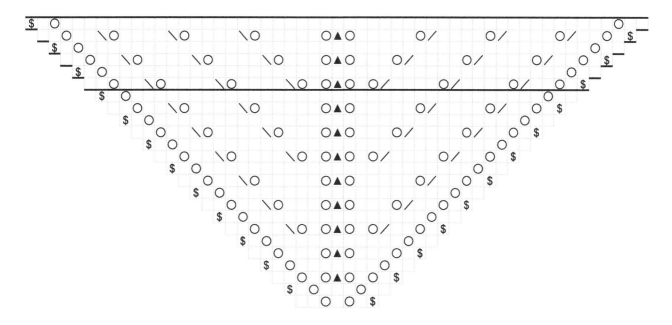

ESTONIAN SQUARE LACE CHART (LARGER)

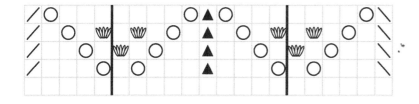

FAROESE SHAWL WING CHART (LARGER)

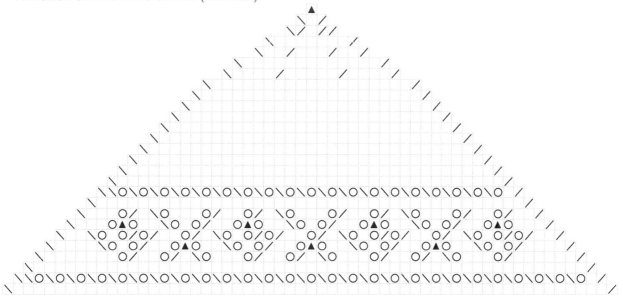

ESTONIAN SQUARE CENTER CHART (LARGER)

TRIANGLE SHAWL CENTER CHART (LARGER)

Making Shawls Your Own

For those who like to play with patterns, many of the centres and laces of the shawls can be changed. Work out the stitch and row repeat and substitute your favourite patterns, perhaps those from my book, *The Magic of Shetland Lace Knitting*.

Borders can also be changed, and laces can be added or not used, as well as being changed.

Here are 'empty charts' for you to photocopy to design with. In each case the essential increases and/or decreases are noted, but the rest is a blank page. Just make sure you have the same number of stitches decreased per row as there are yarn-overs.

Please note that lace charts are not shown as these can vary in width, and different laces have different increasing and decreasing on their outer edge.

Empty charts start on page 85.

Making Mini Shawls Bigger

Although this is a book of patterns for mini shawls, many of them can be made into full sized shawls. Using thicker yarn and bigger needles will always result in a bigger shawl, but with a small amount of number crunching, many can easily be made into full sized shawls using the same needles and yarn as the minis.

I have divided the shawls into three categories: those which are very easy to adapt, those which need a bit of moths and those which will involve more calculations or fudging.

GROUP A: JUST KEEP KNITTING

These minis are easy to make bigger by just keeping on knitting until the piece is big enough, or you run out of yarn. As you knit, look for the places in the pattern where you can stop knitting. If desired, you can add a few rows of garter stitch to finish the shawl off.

GROUP B: STRAIGHTFORWARD MATHS NEEDED

For these shawls extra repeats can be added, and the main calculations needed are adding on a certain number of stitches and rows. They extras needed are given for each shawl.

END TO END CRESCENT SHAWL (p 28)

Add extra pattern repeats to each of the three sections - increase, straight and decrease. As a rule of thumb, use one-third of your yarn for the increase section, one-third for the straight section and one-third for the decrease.

SHORT ROW CRESCENT SHAWL (p 29)

Knit more lace repeats, then pick up the loops along the straight edge. Work out how many stitches you have, and divide by two. From this number, take away 10, and the number you are left with is the number to slip on to the right hand needle. Finish the pattern as written. For example, if you has 120 sts, half of this is 60. Take 10 from 60 and you have 50. So slip 50 sts on to the right hand needle.

SQUARE SHAWL WITH LACE (p 32)

Add multiples of 12 sts and 24 rows to the centre. Each 12 sts/24 rows will need 3 extra lace repeats on each side.

STOLE WITH LACE (p 33)

To make it wider, add multiples of 30 stitches. To make it longer, just keep knitting to the required length before adding the top lace.

TWO-TAIL STOLE (p 35)

To make it wider, add multiples of 10 sts. To make it longer, knit each tail to half the required length before grafting.

WEDGE CIRCLULAR SHAWL (p 41)

To make the shawl bigger needs a longer wedge, increasing at the same rate as before, and finishing with a multiple of 6 sts. The same chart can be used to make a semi-circle, using 4 wedges per row, and adding 2 knit sts at the start and finish of each row as a border.

PI MINI SHAWL (p 43)

The Pi can be made smaller by removing the last section, or made bigger by continuing the process of doubling the number of rows as you double the number of stitches.

SEMI CIRCULAR SHAWL (p 44)

To increase the size is complex, but the chart can be used 7 times per row as a circle.

SHETLAND "INSIDE-OUT" SHAWL (p 46)

The centre can be enlarged by multiples of 20 sts and 40 rows. The border will need one 20st repeat of the middle section for each 20 st/40 row repeat of the centre. The lace will have to be fudged at the corners.

ESTONIAN SQUARE SHAWL (p 52)

The centre can be increased by multiples of 28 sts and 24 rows. For every 28 sts.24 row repeat, each piece of the lace will need 60 extra sts.

ESTONIAN TRIANGLE (p 54)

Just keep knitting extra repeats of the centre, then add a few garter stitch rows at the top to give a multiple of 6 loops for each border. For the border, repeat the 6 sts of the border motif, and the first 12 rows of the border chart as necessary.

FAROESE SHAWL (p 61)

Add multiples of 12 sts to each wing and fudge the gusset. If you are going to add more than 12 sts to each wing, double the gusset chart at the cast on edge and work out the placings of the decreases before you start.

STAR WASH CLOTH (p 65)

Continue increasing the centre as before until the main part of the shawl is the right size. Then decrease in each point in the same way as for the mini.

BOOKMARK (p 69)

For a narrow scarf just keep knitting in thicker yarn on bigger needles until the scarf is the right size. To make the piece wider, add multiples of 14 sts, having a knit stitch between the motifs.

TRIANGLE SHAWL (p 72)

Keep repeating the centre chart as required, then add 10 sts to the border for every extra repeat of the centre.

GROUP C: COMPLEX

Enlarging these shawls will involve a fair bit of maths, as the stitch and row repeats of the centres, borders and laces do not easily match. But anyone who is confident with a calculator and the idea of fudging will be able to make the changes needed.

85

EMPTY FISCHOU

EVERY ROW CHARTED

* Can also be used for a tip up triangle as 'alternate rows only charted,' ignoring the $ at the end of the rows.

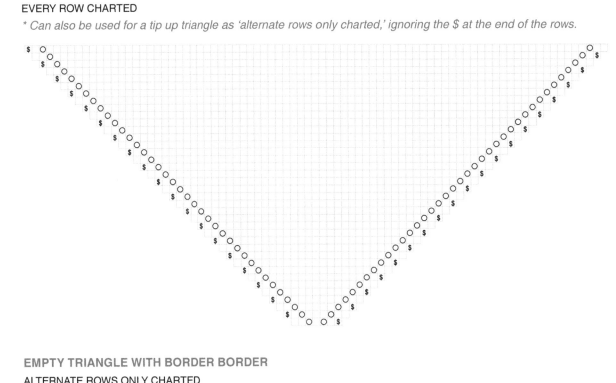

EMPTY TRIANGLE WITH BORDER BORDER

ALTERNATE ROWS ONLY CHARTED

EMPTY TRIANGLE WITH BORDER CENTRE

ALTERNATE ROWS ONLY CHARTED

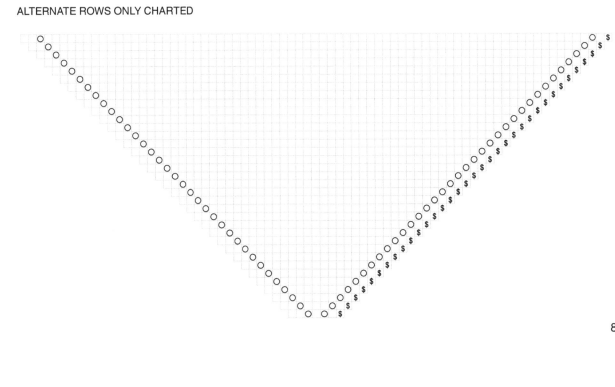

EMPTY FAROESE GUSSET
ALTERNATE ROWS ONLY CHARTED

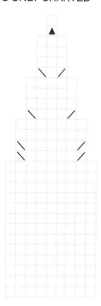

EMPTY SHETLAND OUTSIDE IN LACE CORNER
EVERY ROW CHARTED

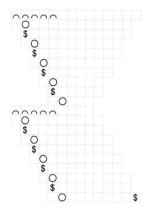

EMPTY SHETLAND OUTSIDE IN LACE
EVERY ROW CHARTED

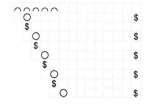

EMPTY FAROESE WING
ALTERNATE ROWS ONLY CHARTED

EMPTY SHETLAND INSIDE OUT BORDER

ALTERNATE ROWS ONLY CHARTED

EMPTY SHETLAND OUTSIDE IN BORDER

EVERY ROW CHARTED

EMPTY SHETLAND INSIDE OUT CENTRE
ALTERNATE ROWS ONLY CHARTED

EMPTY SHETLAND INSIDE OUT LACE
EVERY ROW CHARTED

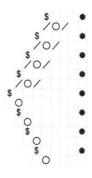

EMPTY SHETLAND OUTSIDE IN CENTRE
EVERY ROW CHARTED

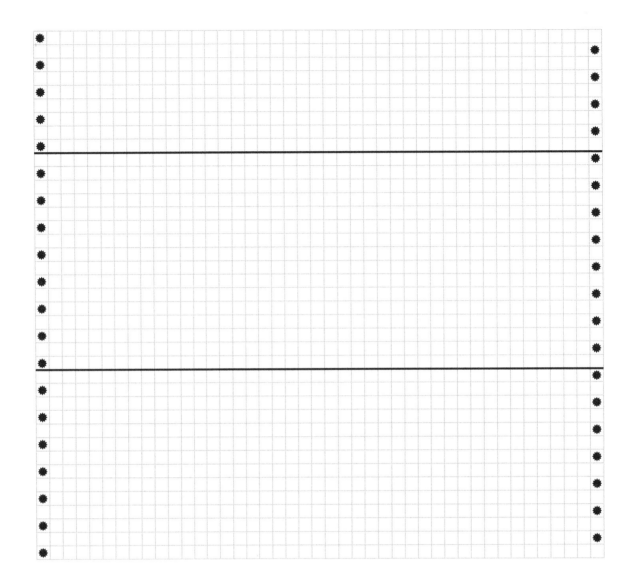

EMPTY WEDGE FOR CIRCLE OR SEMI-CIRCLE
ALTERNATE ROWS ONLY CHARTED

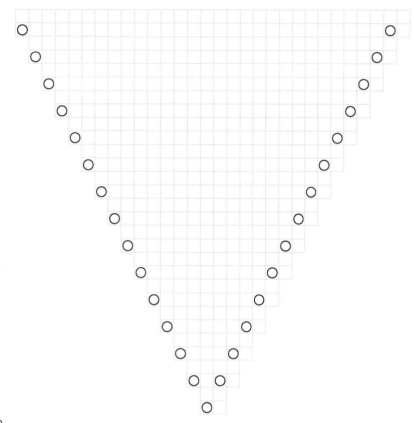

EMPTY SPIRAL CIRCLE
ALTERNATE ROWS ONLY CHARTED

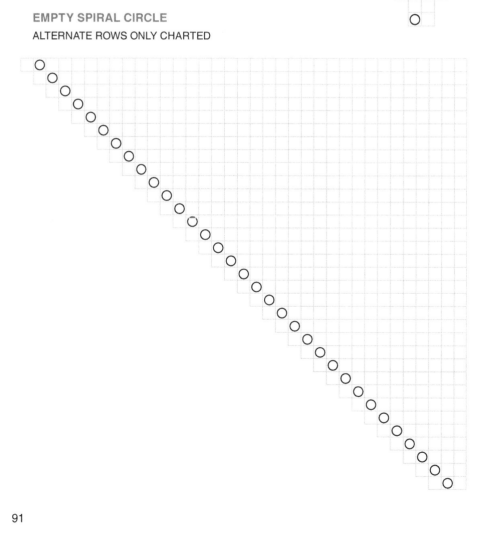

Northern Lace Press

Flotta – Orkney – Scotland

Fair Isle Workbook

Elizabeth Lovick
Northern Lace Press Workbook Series #1

http://northernlacepress.co.uk

Fair Isle Workbook
(Workbook Series #1)
978-0-9930614-2-4

The workbook is arranged in separate 'lessons' including detailed instructions with lots of clear photos of topics such as ways to hold the yarns, steeking and dealing with mistakes. Throughout the book the emphasis is on helping you to understand how Fair Isle knitting 'works' and aims to give you the confidence not only to knit other people's patterns, but to chart your own and work out your own colour schemes. The book includes a pattern for the traditional Ha'af cap and a beanie, with charts for a wide variety of alternative designs.

Gansey Workbook
(Workbook Series #2)
978-0-9930614-3-1

Ganseys are working sweaters worn by fishermen around the coasts of the UK. Arranged in the form of 'lessons', it explains the techniques particular to ganseys and gives patterns for various small items There are several pages of charts of motifs from different parts of the UK and hints on how to use them to design your own gansey. The book includes history of ganseys and includes a tour round the British coast showing the typical patterns used in different areas. It ends with a 5 ply gansey pattern in many sizes.

Northern Lace Press

Flotta – Orkney – Scotland

Gansey Workbook

Elizabeth Lovick
Northern Lace Press Workbook Series #2

http://northernlacepress.co.uk

Fine Spinning Workbook
(Workbook Series #3)

978-0-9930614-4-8

Ways to spin fine and ultra fine yarns on spindles and wheels. The workbook consists of 42 pages of detailed theory and practise, illustrated with photos throughout, and arranged in 'lessons'. It is suitable for anyone who can already spin a thread – you do not have to be an expert when you start! In each lesson you will move from the theory to the practise, ending with exercises to help your progress. There is a large section on trouble shooting. A triangular mini shawl pattern is included.

Northern Lace Press

Fine Spinning Workbook

Flotta – Orkney – Scotland

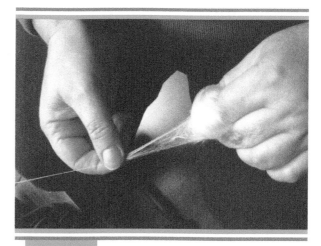

Elizabeth Lovick
Northern Lace Press Workbook Series #3

http://northernlacepress.co.uk

Northern Lace Press

Knitwear Design
for Spinners and Knitters

Flotta – Orkney – Scotland

Elizabeth Lovick
Northern Lace Press Workbook Series #4

http://northernlacepress.co.uk

Knitwear Design
for Spinners and Knitters
(Workbook Series #4)

978-0-9930614-5-5

This book starts with a section for spinners looking at how best to spin yarn for a specific project. It then goes on to talk about things you need to consider when designing. Throughout there are many photos, using examples in all areas of knitting. There is then a comprehensive chapter on ways to get round mistakes. After the general section, there are chapters on lace and colour work design, including talking through the real process of designing an actual garment.

Full information can be found at
http://northernlacepress.co.uk

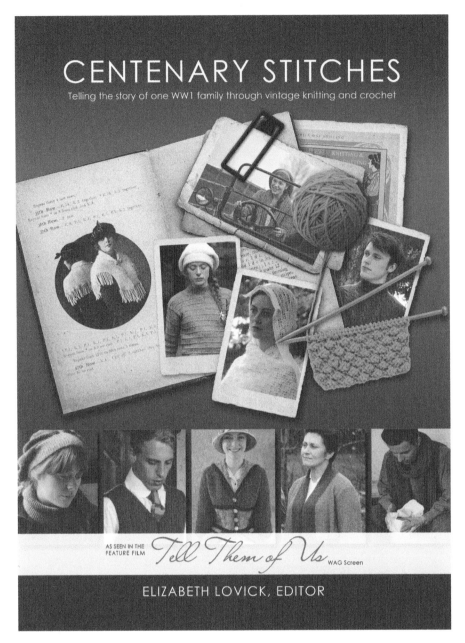

CENTENARY STITCHES

Telling the story of one WW1 family through vintage knitting and crochet

AS SEEN IN THE FEATURE FILM *Tell Them of Us* WAG Screen

ELIZABETH LOVICK, EDITOR

160 pages, full colour • More than 70 patterns • Also available as an ebook.

Includes articles about the Crowder family, the village of Thimbleby, and the making of the film.

Full information can be found at http://northernlacepress.co.uk

Northern Lace Press

Flotta — Orkney — Scotland

Acknowledgements

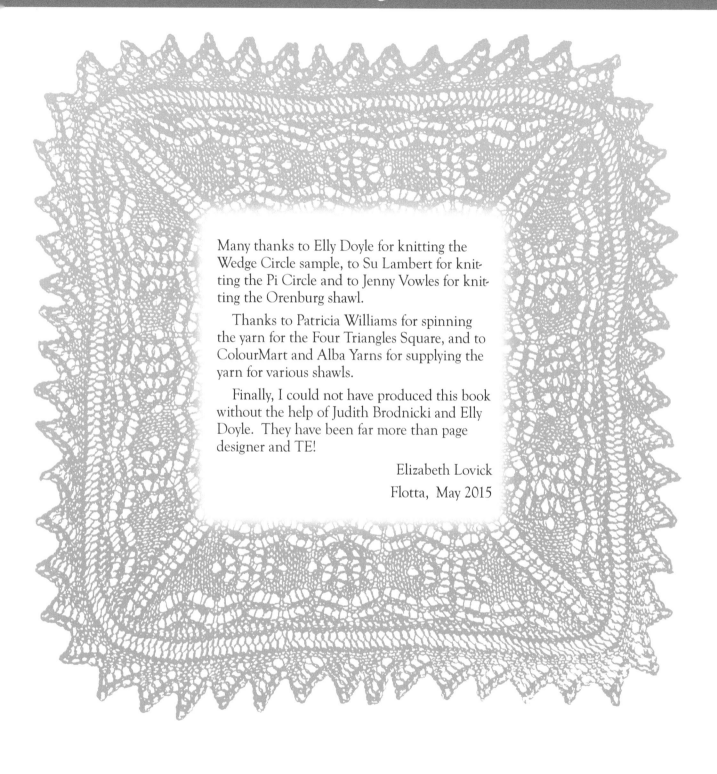

Many thanks to Elly Doyle for knitting the Wedge Circle sample, to Su Lambert for knitting the Pi Circle and to Jenny Vowles for knitting the Orenburg shawl.

Thanks to Patricia Williams for spinning the yarn for the Four Triangles Square, and to ColourMart and Alba Yarns for supplying the yarn for various shawls.

Finally, I could not have produced this book without the help of Judith Brodnicki and Elly Doyle. They have been far more than page designer and TE!

Elizabeth Lovick

Flotta, May 2015

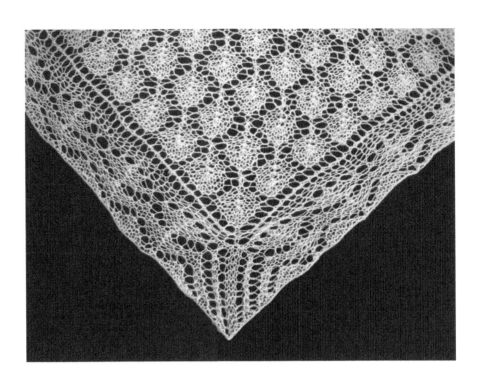

ELIZABETH LOVICK (author, knitter, designer, historian) was taught to knit by her Cornish grandmother when very young and kept herself in clothes through school by knitting arans for friends! She lives and works on the small Orkney island of Flotta where she spins and knits, researches and writes. She is the author of *The Magic of Shetland Lace Knitting* and editor of *Centenary Stitches: Telling the Story of a WW1 Family through Knitting and Crochet*.

Elly Doyle (technical editor, knitter) moved to Orkney a year ago after living in the Faroe Islands. She is a self-confessed 'numbers person' and enjoys the detail of technical editing. As a designer she specialises in colourwork accessories; as a dyer she specialises in the fibre of the local North Ronaldsay sheep.

Judith Brodnicki (graphic designer, knitter) has more than 25 years of experience in print production and graphic design. Her patterns are published on Knitty, Ravelry, and Knit Picks web sites. She lives in Omaha, Nebraska, with her husband, 2 dogs and 2 cats.

Lightning Source UK Ltd.
Milton Keynes UK
UKOW07f0612030915

258007UK00005B/24/P